Lena loo[...]

There was no way you could mistake this man for anything other than a leader, but there was more to it than that. Gabe was a man so beautiful it almost hurt your eyes to look at him. Nothing about him was out of place. His looks alone would be enough to garner a following if that were the audience the family was after.

Of course, she'd done her research. She knew about his work. His past as a junior football player leading his country to an international championship. There was another story, one in the past. That was the sort of thing that people could get excited about. Even her blood had pumped a bit harder and the room had gotten strangely warm when she looked at the photographs of that long-ago win. But where had that man gone? Disappeared under the weight of his role? It was hard to tell. Though one thing was clear, the future of the royal family was this man in front of her.

*A brand-new and royally captivating duet
from Harlequin Presents author Kali Anthony!*

Royal House of Halrovia

One royal family, two matches fit for the crown...

Royal siblings Crown Prince Gabriel and
Princess Anastacia have had their unfair share of
scandalous headlines. Courting the press has been
essential! And in a family where every move is
scrutinized, they need all the help they can get
to keep up their royal appearances...

Anastacia was always the perfect princess,
until an accident threw her whole world into disarray.
To quell the rumors, she's forced to accept a proposal
from Aston Lane—the charming billionaire who makes
her heart race! And falling for her convenient fiancé
might be Ana's riskiest move yet...

Read Ana's story in
Royal Fiancée Required

Crown Prince Gabriel has sacrificed everything
for his country. So with the monarchy's popularity
plummeting, he has to find a way to reach his people—
fast! Enter PR expert Lena Rosetti. Only, the off-limits
attraction between them is out of control enough
to force Gabe to choose—between his duty...
and his desire!

Discover Gabe's story in
Prince She Shouldn't Crave

Both available now!

PRINCE SHE SHOULDN'T CRAVE

KALI ANTHONY

PRESENTS

Harlequin®
PRESENTS™

ISBN-13: 978-1-335-21315-0

Prince She Shouldn't Crave

Copyright © 2025 by Kali Anthony

Recycling programs for this product may not exist in your area.

Harlequin Enterprises ULC
22 Adelaide St. West, 41st Floor
Toronto, Ontario M5H 4E3, Canada
www.Harlequin.com

Printed in Lithuania

MIX
Paper | Supporting responsible forestry
FSC® C021394

When **Kali Anthony** read her first romance novel at fourteen, she realized a few truths: there can never be too many happy endings, and one day she would write them herself. After marrying her own tall, dark and handsome hero in a perfect friends-to-lovers romance, Kali took the plunge and penned her first story. Writing has been a love affair ever since. If she isn't battling her cat for access to the keyboard, you can find Kali playing dress-up in vintage clothes, gardening or bushwhacking with her husband and three children in the rainforests of South East Queensland.

Books by Kali Anthony

Harlequin Presents

Revelations of His Runaway Bride
Bound as His Business-Deal Bride
Off-Limits to the Crown Prince
Snowbound in His Billion-Dollar Bed
Awoken by Revenge

Behind the Palace Doors...

The Marriage That Made Her Queen
Engaged to London's Wildest Billionaire
Crowned for the King's Secret

Royal House of Halrovia

Royal Fiancée Required

Visit the Author Profile page
at Harlequin.com.

To Lissanne, friend, author bestie and
fellow lover of royal romance. Thank you for helping
me stay on track and motivated, and being there
in the hard times as well as the fun ones.
Here's to many more royal romances between us.

CHAPTER ONE

GABRIEL MONTROY SLIPPED a monogrammed gold cufflink into the pristine white cuff of his shirt. Clipped it into place, tugged at one sleeve, then the other, adjusting them both. He glanced at a few of the more odious Halrovian tabloids tossed carelessly on a coffee table in his personal suite, the stark black headlines meaningless patterns against the dusky paper. He didn't have the time or the energy to try reading them this morning.

'What do they say today, Pieter?'

His valet sniffed.

'The same as ever, Your Highness. No worse, no better.'

That didn't bode well. Whilst the more traditional media remained staunch supporters of the Montroy royal family, over the past year something in the tabloids had turned. Morphing from overblown yet generally benign commentary to something darker, nastier. Once, he'd agreed with his parents about ignoring them, in a time where the news stories had tended to be more about titillation than truth. Then they'd evolved from being an irritating mosquito that could be quelled with a swat, to a venomous spider weaving a toxic web of lies...

Gabe did up the top button of his shirt, slowly fastening

himself into place. His valet handed him a gleaming silk tie. 'The darker blue today, sir. I believe it conveys a sense of leadership, without appearing overtly intimidating.'

Gabe had no interest in colour theory, or whatever Pieter called it. He was Crown Prince of Halrovia. A position that was to be upheld with authority and confidence. His family was supposed to be the country's bedrock. Him, its fresh foundation. Instead, the press seemed intent on rumour and innuendo. More recently about his sisters, and now him. Heir apparent to the Montroy Crown. Once dubbed the Proper Prince, that moniker now used to disparage rather than to praise.

Something needed to change in the way his image was managed. Whereas his parents and their press secretary wanted everything to stay the same, he recognised that now was not the time to play safe. They—*he*—needed to take a risk. He'd known what that was like once. He'd been all about the risk and resulting reward. Gabe wasn't sure why the thought had his heart pumping as if he'd run down a football field, the opposition chasing him down. Attempting to tackle him as he made his way to the goal...

Gabriel tried to ignore the sensation, that frisson of a memory. Those days were long behind him. Instead he lifted his collar and draped the tie around his neck, tying it in a knot. Tightening it, adjusting it. Loosening it a fraction. It had begun to feel like a noose. Yet there was no point to these thoughts. He'd accepted the price he'd had to pay for those days as captain of Halrovia's national under-twenty-one's football team. When he'd lived life a little too full. Been justifiably cocky, untouchable, until he'd trusted someone who hadn't deserved the privilege.

He shrugged on his jacket, then turned to the mirror. Tugging his shirtsleeves again so his cuffs sat perfectly even, his persona firmly in place. He took a deep, slow breath, allowing himself to remember, and in some ways regret, the innocence and ignorance of his late teens.

'Read me *one*. The most egregious.'

His valet walked to the coffee table, sifted through a few of the papers as if there were something dirty on them.

'"*Are Minor Scandals Hinting at Bigger Secrets? The Nation Wonders...*"'

Any scandals were wishful thinking in the minds of the tabloid's editors. Secrets, however... He'd held on to his own since childhood. Was protected by his parents when its disclosure threatened the myth of perfection that was his family.

'That headline doesn't meet the definition of egregious.'

'In the sub-heading there's talk of a palace source expressing concerns that opinion ratings of the royal family are falling, which might lead the public to clamour for a... *republic*.'

Pieter almost spat out the word as if it were spoiled food in his mouth.

'Which is why I have a plan to reverse that alleged sentiment.'

'Then I trust the interview goes well, sir.'

Gabe nodded. Slipped in some earbuds, grabbed his mobile phone and opened the text-to-speech app, listening once again to the CV his private secretary had downloaded for him as he made his way to his palace office. Someone to manage his image, since giving his youth and his life working for the crown didn't seem to be enough.

He shut down the prickle of resentment at that thought and concentrated on the history and achievements of the person he was about to interview. Someone recommended by his sister, Priscilla. Last on the list, after he'd seen and discounted several polished but uninspiring candidates. Cilla raved about the woman who'd worked with her for around nine months on PR and the social media accounts of the Isolobello royal family, after Cilla moved there following her engagement to their Crown Prince. He wasn't so enthusiastic. Whilst her references were impressive, any tertiary studies were mysteriously absent.

Just like you.

He ignored that voice as he pushed through the doors of his office, checking the time. His situation was different. What he needed was someone to impress him. As he looked around a waiting area, he saw no one but his private secretary, Henri.

'She's late,' Gabe said.

Strike one, if he was looking for reasons not to hire the woman. He was *never* late. In Gabe's view, a lack of punctuality was a result of poor planning and lack of consideration.

'If it's any consolation, sir, she called sounding suitably panicked. It seemed genuine, and Security tell me she has arri—'

The door to the anteroom burst open. Gabe and his secretary turned as in rushed a whirlwind in black and white. A woman, grappling an overstuffed handbag as she hauled it up her shoulder and straightened her jacket, before stilling as if some forest creature caught in a hunter's sights. Her ocean-blue gaze connected with his, her eyes widening. The shock of that vivid colour trapped him, and he couldn't look away. Then he caught her scent, like hot chocolate and spice. It teased his senses, made his mouth water as if she might be the perfect dessert, which of course was nonsensical. Then a strange heat burst inside his chest, radiating outwards. He had the irresistible desire to tug at his tie and loosen it further as the room grew too warm.

What the hell? Perhaps he should get his private secretary to check the air-conditioning.

'I—I...' The woman glanced from him to his private secretary and back again.

'Your Highness,' Henri said with a quizzical kind of look on his face. 'Ms Lena Rosetti.'

Ms Rosetti seemed to compose herself. She dipped into a deep and perfect curtsey. His body's reaction was immediate and brutal, like a kick to the solar plexus. A physical blow he required all his years of royal training to not show, and that was even before his mind had really registered the full sense of her rather than the parts he'd first noticed. Her fathomless eyes. Her intoxicating perfume.

The picture then began to click into place, almost as if his brain were putting her together like a jigsaw puzzle. There was nothing outstanding about her appearance. A black suit. Shop bought, because he *knew* tailoring, but nicely fitted. Her jacket buttoned up high, crisp white shirt, dull flat shoes that looked out of place with the outfit. Black hair pulled back in a severe bun. Totally unremarkable, except for her eyes, and yet he was like a tuning fork just struck. He vibrated.

'We have a problem.'

The words simply spilled out of him with no thought to his illogical reaction to her. Her soft pink mouth opened into a perfect O. She reached up her hand almost as a reflex as if to tuck some stray hair behind her ear. Ms Rosetti had long, elegant fingers, though why that observation was of any consequence he couldn't say. Then she seemed to hesitate, as if realising there was no stray hair to be put back into place. Instead, she rustled about her handbag. Tugged something out, held it up.

'I broke a heel.'

He was assailed by her voice, its softness, like a caress. The melodic sound of her accent signalled she was from the country of Isolobello with its Latin roots, being an island state off the coast of Italy. Where his sister Cilla now lived, and would become future Queen when she married Prince Caspar in a number of months.

Luckily Ms Rosetti was oblivious to the sensations warring inside him, or that his words had been meant to convey another meaning entirely. That it wasn't her lateness, but his reaction to her, that was the real issue. Then he looked at what she held in her hand. A stiletto. Black. Patent leather. The type of shoe that would make the calves of any woman wearing it swell in a distracting kind of way. Heels seductively lengthening her legs.

The type of shoes a man might ask a woman to leave on, not take off.

Gabe tried to ignore the burn of heat that once again roared over him. Instead, he concentrated on the broken heel that was, indeed, dangling from the shoe.

A faint wash of colour drifted across her cheeks. Did something show on his face? The strange desire that hit like a kick in the gut again? He needed to rein it in. Time he'd been spending trying to quell the negative press had meant a case of all work and no play. Though for Gabe, since his early twenties, any amount of 'play' had always been intensely discreet. He'd been taught a painful lesson of what might occur if you let the wrong person get too close. The ideas that fertile imaginations could conjure. Now, he had a firm rule. Don't subject a woman to the glare of the spotlight unnecessarily if she was never going to be his wife.

'Put the footwear away, Ms Rosetti. I demand punctuality of my employees, and of myself.'

'It's why I was late. I—I twisted my ankle on the cobblestones on the way and had to find alternative shoes.' She looked down at her feet and his gaze followed. She seemed to wiggle her toes in her uninspiringly practical flat shoes, but his attention locked on her elegant slender ankles. Ones that his hands might encircle easily.

This wouldn't do. What he needed was to contact one of the few friends with benefits he kept. Women who enjoyed pleasure for the evening and would go on their way. No expectations from either of them. He knew there was a certain cache in the aristocracy with being his lover, even if it would never come to anything. All he needed to do was make a call. Engage in an evening of mutual, adult pleasure.

He had no idea why, right now, that thought held no interest. Yet the recesses of his errant brain finally registered her words. Had she hurt herself? What was he thinking? Nothing sensible at all, clearly.

'Do you require medical attention?'

She shook her head. 'No, thank you, sir.'

He strangely liked the way she called him sir, even though all his staff used the term. What would it be like to hear her say his name? Gabriel... Gabe.

Impossible.

This was meant to be an interview. An audition of sorts, but not one for a lover.

'Come into my office. Take a seat.'

He turned and led the way. Trying to ignore the prickle at the back of his neck indicating she was close.

He lowered himself into his own chair. Blue tie be damned. He clasped his hands in front of him. Fixed her with a glare. The one he usually reserved for more recalcitrant advisors of state, which people might describe as *overtly* intimidating. She was to be in charge of his *image*. One that was very personal to him. Further, anyone who worked so closely with him might come to know secrets. Some he'd prefer weren't exposed.

'One hint. I value punctuality...'

'But—'

He held up his hand. She stopped speaking. '...and preparedness.'

'So do I,' she shot straight back, then seemed to pull into herself. Adjusted her shapely jacket, which remained buttoned closed.

'I'm a reasonable employer. However, I have high expectations.'

She nodded. Short, sharp and businesslike. 'I understand.'

'Excellent. Then let's begin. I have questions.' So many questions. Whilst she came highly recommended, she seemed underqualified for the role. 'You've read the brief?'

To improve his relatability. One day he'd rule the country. Need to make hard and sometimes impossible decisions. To do that required inner strength...steel. None of it would be helped by him effectively being a 'nice guy' about it.

'Of course. I have a question of my own, if I may?'

His eyebrows rose. She liked to think she could take charge here? Something about the challenge of it all set his pulse rate thumping like he'd just taken a run.

'Be my guest,' he said, injecting a warning note of dryness into his voice.

She seemed to ignore his tone as she rummaged about her bag and pulled out a tablet. Flicked through a few screens and drew up some photographs, then slid it across the desktop to him.

'I think this is who you need to show the world. My question for you is, where is this person?'

Gabe looked at the pictures on the screen. The rapid hum of his heart stilled. Photographs of him a long time ago, from his late teens and into twenty. An ache bloomed deep inside his chest. Holding the world championship cup aloft, yellow and blue confetti in colours of Halrovia's flag fluttering down over him and his team as they celebrated their win. Shots of him out somewhere, leaving some function. Smiling for the cameras in a way that seemed totally unfamiliar. A young woman on his arm.

That woman… The press speculation had been intense but she'd wanted so much more from him than he could ever have given. A daughter of an aristocrat who clearly had expectations of a royal future, her family too, when all he'd wanted was… Gabe hadn't been sure. To be seen as something more? His difficulty reading had crippled him at school. For so long Gabe had been thought of as lazy, he'd begun to believe he would never make a decent king when it was his time. Never achieving what his parents or teachers had expected of him.

Then came the diagnosis, yet the only result from the King and Queen was steely silence. His dyslexia barely talked about, efficiently swept under the ancient rugs of the royal palace. And so he talked, not to his family, but to the person he thought of as his girlfriend, even if he hadn't contemplated any real future with her. Then, when that youthful relationship came to its inevitable end, after her tears, the threats started. That she'd tell everyone he'd be a useless king because he couldn't read. Had she and her family believed she might be Queen one day and been trying to blackmail him into reversing the break-up? He couldn't be sure. All he knew was his parents and the royal machine surrounding them took her threats seriously.

He didn't want to think about the consequences of that time because he and his family were still living them. The steps his parents took to quell the rumours. The prices paid. Some by his family, mostly by him. Forgoing the life he'd wanted for one of duty, so nobody could question his commitment to the crown. Especially if he spent all his time learning from his father how to be King.

In that time, the Proper Prince was born.

Still, these weren't conversations he would deign to have with a person he hadn't yet decided to employ.

'He grew up,' Gabriel said, pushing the tablet back towards her, dismissing the unwanted memories. 'Now for my questions.'

Time to bring this interview back under his tight control. Ms Rosetti didn't seem to be put off. She straightened herself, tugged at her jacket and her jaw firmed, as if preparing for some kind of battle.

He couldn't help but admire her resolve.

'You have no university qualifications in marketing, PR or social media. Yet you're asking me to trust you with what some see as the future of my family in the eyes of its people.' Lena Rosetti sat perfectly still. The only give-away? The slender line of her neck convulsed in a swallow. 'What makes you believe you can provide me with value that's superior, when I have other candidates who are formally qualified?'

Lena's heart punched into her ribs. She swallowed, damp palms clutching at the leather of her handbag still sitting on her lap. Questioning some of her life choices. Why had she decided to be forward and show him those photographs of himself? Why had she shown him her *shoe*? In her defence she was a little overwhelmed because, in the flesh, Prince Gabriel looked too good to be entirely human. Sure, she'd seen plenty of photos of him during her research. But no picture could do him real justice. He was almost supernaturally handsome, in a way that turned her normally quite functional brain to custard. If gods walked the earth, she reckoned they'd look just like Prince Gabriel.

Which was her reminder, he wasn't a god but a man. Who'd apparently *'grown up'* and *'valued punctuality'*. He wouldn't care about her broken heel. It was obvious by the way he'd looked at her when she'd pulled it out of her handbag, as if that would have helped when trying to explain why she was late. The sheer intensity of his gaze had made her go all hot and cold and every temperature in between. That look in his eyes speaking of what?

Disdain. She was sure.

Lena was used to that look, back in her home country of

Isolobello. Had fought against it for most of her twenty-three years. It was how so many people at her exclusive private school had looked at her for the temerity of being father-less. Oh, she'd had a father. An absent one. A high-profile one. A man never named, publicly at least. That had been the arrangement. He'd kept her mother in a lifestyle she'd become accustomed to for all the years of their long-term affair. He'd kept his second family, the illegitimate family, in the shadows. Secret from everybody.

Then he'd died just three months earlier. Suddenly. Shockingly. Soon after, their life had imploded. The half-brother she'd never met had arrived on their doorstep stating that 'the gravy train', as he so crudely had put it, was over. Her mother could keep her jewels and whatever gifts she'd been given during her father's life and that was all. Her father hadn't recognised her family in his will. As far as the legitimate family was concerned, Lena, her mother and her brother didn't exist. The sour taste of bile rose to Lena's throat. He'd said they were a dirty stain on a great man's legacy.

Which was why she *needed* this role. Lena's whole fu-ture relied on it. To keep her younger brother in education so he could make something of himself. To support her mother so she wouldn't end up destitute, on the street. And if she didn't pull herself together, it seemed as if it might slip through her fingers.

'I'd hoped my references spoke for themselves. Each em-ployer I've worked for showed an increase in business due to my efforts.'

Prince Gabriel narrowed his eyes. 'That may be so, yet your career didn't start in managing people's images and

PR. You seem to have fallen into the role by chance rather than design.'

'There is a divinity that shapes our ends, rough-hew them how we will.'

A quote from Shakespeare, often used by one of her favourite teachers, a woman whose wisdom she missed. Especially when her mother's idea for solving their current crisis was for Lena to find a wealthy man and either advantageously marry or become a well-cared-for mistress, just as she'd been, and provide for the family. Her mother had even named possible males who might be in the market.

The prospect of this job had fallen into her lap at exactly the right time. The universe was telling her the role was hers, she just needed to secure it.

'You're correct. In my first job I was employed to wait café tables, but my employer asked me to post some pictures on social media. Their page became hugely popular and people started flooding to the café because of the vibe we showed them on the social channels.'

She was only nineteen when she started that job. One her mother said she didn't need, but Lena had wanted anyhow. To have money and something of her own, not handed to her by an absent father. Lena got a buzz from how big the café's page had become, how customers came in because they'd seen *her* posts. But what she'd said didn't seem to impress Prince Gabriel. He raised one strong, dark eyebrow. A contrast to his hair, which was a magnificent, tamed mane of burnished gold.

'And yet should you succeed in this interview you'd be managing more than my...vibe.'

His image and his 'vibe' were kind of the same thing,

in her opinion anyhow, but she wasn't about to disagree with him.

'My next job was more intentional.' A florist and gift shop supporting local artisans from Isolobello. Whilst working in the gift shop there, Lena had suggested a bigger social media presence. Posting pictures of the glorious blooms. Featuring the work of various creators. 'Through my efforts, their business became extremely popular and drew the attention of your sister, who'd come into the store *because* she'd seen my posts on social media showcasing my employer's values in supporting lesser-known artists.'

'I believe the person you're meaning to refer to, Ms Rosetti, is *Princess Priscilla*.'

'Of course, Your Highness.'

Heat crept up her neck, prickling where the tag of her loathsome black jacket scratched her skin. She tugged at the collar, but that didn't seem to help much. Lena found it hard to think of Prince Gabriel's sister as a princess. *Cilla*, as she'd demanded to be called within five minutes of meeting Lena, didn't care one bit about royal titles. They'd quickly struck up an easy kind of friendship. When Lena decided it was time to move on from her job in the florist's, Cilla had suggested a role in Isolobello's palace as a junior in their social media and PR department.

'Would you care to remove your jacket, Ms Rosetti?' Prince Gabriel asked. His voice deep and rich like the hot chocolate she loved to drink as a treat when something had gone well. 'Whilst this is a professional workplace, they're not always required.'

She didn't believe him. This man looked so tightly buttoned up she'd almost bet that he'd have to be cut out of his suit each evening. Then, each morning, a new one would be stitched right back onto his fine, *fine* body.

Fine body? Where had *that* thought come from?

'Thank you, n-no. I—I'm quite comfortable.'

She was anything but. And although she wanted to accept his invitation and tear off her jacket with every fibre of her existence, she couldn't. On the way to the palace, she'd had a cup of coffee, hoping the caffeine would give her a bit of a boost. She should have known that wearing a white shirt was an invitation to spill something on it. If she took off her jacket now, His Royal Highness would see a good portion of her shirt indelibly stained, because of her clumsiness. Something her mother always complained about.

'You're as elegant as a newborn donkey. Glide, Lena. Glide like a swan.'

Lena bet her mother had never seen a newborn donkey. Yet she shouldn't be thinking about spilled coffee or stuttering or blushing. She should be answering his questions. This job was a stepping stone to securing her family's future. To even bigger, better things.

Lena took a steadying breath. She knew how to do this. She'd prepared for it, the possible questions. The answers she needed to give.

'Earlier, sir, you pointed out my lack of university qualifications. I respect a formal education.' More than respected it, she'd craved it, had seen it as a way to avoid what had befallen her beautiful, unqualified mother. Her parents hadn't seen the point of a degree in PR and marketing, suggesting something like art history which Lena had no interest in. But they'd finally capitulated after she simply applied to her university of choice and been accepted, even if she had started her degree far later than her peers. When Lena had been forced to give up her own studies after her father had died, it had been a crushing sacrifice. 'However, the job you're asking me to do requires creativity, and a deep understanding of the audience you're trying to connect with. As I assess the role, I *am* the audience. You're trying to connect with someone like *me*.'

Prince Gabriel cocked his head. Narrowed his gaze. She felt skewered to the spot. Rather like a butterfly pinned to a board by an icicle.

'Am I, Ms Rosetti?'

Lena froze. Did she really say that? Him, *connecting* with her? What was she thinking? The truth was, not much at all. Everything about him seemed so intentional and planned that he discombobulated her. His frigid blue tie matching icy blue eyes that the Montroy family were famed for. His shirt, white like hers, but unmarred by coffee. Impeccably pressed. Not a wrinkle to be seen. In fact, no wrinkle would *dare*. He was so perfect she was terrified that if she got too close her clumsiness would overwhelm her and she'd somehow manage to spill something on him, like the untouched mug that was sitting on his desk.

Yet if she allowed herself to be distracted by all of this— all of him—she'd fail, then where would she be left? She didn't want a relationship like her mother had had, or a marriage to some rich man who sought her out because of her age, her looks and—if they found out—her cursed virginity.

Lena shuddered and pulled herself together.

'That's what your brief said. That you're looking at connecting with younger people and I'm young—'

'*How* young?'

'The demographic your job description said you wanted to target is eighteen to twenty-five and I'm twenty-three. I'm at the upper end.'

'And how do you suppose I'm to…connect? You've given me no answers, only more questions as to why you're better than any other potential candidate for the role.'

Lena sat up a bit straighter. Whatever this man thought or said, she was *good* at what she did. And she'd been working informally and then formally in this type of role since her first job. In her favour, Lena also knew what it was like working for royalty. Sure, getting the job with Isolobello's royal family had been more luck rather than planning. As for this job, Cilla had said her brother *needed* someone like Lena. And she'd happily move to Halrovia permanently if it meant a step up in responsibility and income.

'You might recall the announcement of Prince Caspar's engagement. The celebration weekend. Isolobello's Crown Prince finally set to marry.'

Prince Gabriel sat back in his seat, a little more relaxed. The corner of his perfect mouth curling in what threatened to be a smile but never quite made it. She wanted to see him smile and dreaded it all the same, because if he smiled, every available and inclined woman on the planet would become utterly infatuated with him. Give him one shred of warmth and people wouldn't be able to help themselves.

She didn't know why that thought made acid churn in her gut.

'I do recall, given, as you so eloquently put it before, Prince Caspar's fiancée is *my sister*.'

She knew then that he was trying to be…princely. Lena's job was to stop him hiding behind his title and start showing the world Gabriel Montroy, even though it was clear that he wasn't at all keen on the idea.

'My colleagues wanted a more traditional approach. A few formal engagement photos. Talk of the joining of two long-term allies. I thought the moment was more important than that—'

'More important than the hundreds of years of history between the House of Santori and the House of Montroy?'

His voice was as brittle as the first winter ice cracking in spring. It sounded a warning. She ignored it.

'Yes, and Her Royal Highness agreed.'

When Lena had made her pitch about what she'd thought should happen with the royal announcement, no one had been much on board with her suggestions. Except Cilla. She'd been Lena's greatest supporter.

'The event required something more, because it was a story about love,' she said.

So clearly in Lena's mind, since everyone had believed that Prince Caspar had been going to marry Cilla's older sister, Anastacia. Princess Priscilla was a huge surprise, until you saw the couple together. Then you knew. There could be no doubt that theirs was a relationship meant to be.

Lena wasn't looking for a relationship *at all*. She had trouble trusting one. As far as she was concerned, they seemed like a trap after what had happened to her mother, ostensibly for love. Then her father, and how he'd treated his wife. In the end, he'd really betrayed two women. Sure, she'd dabbled at university with a few boys her age when they'd asked her out, but none had appealed because she'd been so focussed on her studies. Then there were the older men who wanted to possess her for no other reason than she was young, and they thought her beautiful. She'd had limited but enough experience of those sorts too. Particularly some customers in one of her jobs. The things said. Notes left for her... Her skin crawled at the memories as if there were spiders trapped underneath. Lena was looking for a future she was in control of. Not one at the behest of a man who supplied fleeting moments of himself, and money, but nothing else.

She was enough. Lena Rosetti, on her own.

All she needed to do was catch this job as if her life depended on it. She narrowed her eyes. There was a role here. She just had to convince Prince Gabriel she was the best person for it.

'Other members of the team all talked about the past. But it was also a story about Isolobello's *future*. I wanted a behind-the-scenes view of the new couple. Featuring the woman who was going to become our queen one day. The royal family's social media sites showed a significant increase in engagement but, most importantly, there was overwhelmingly positive feedback from the younger demographic.'

'I've no great story about love or any betrothal to improve the Montroy royal family's metrics. *My* future is about ensuring *Halrovia's* future.'

'But everyone has a story. You just need to know how to tell a good one.'

You need me...

Where had that thought come from? She was manifesting, that was all. Taking what his sister had said and running with it.

Prince Gabriel sat back in his chair, held his arms out. 'How would you tell mine, *better*?'

He had such an aura of authority. There was no way you could mistake this man for anything other than a leader but there was more to it than that. It almost hurt your eyes to look at him, he was so imposing, so…breathtaking. His looks alone would be enough to garner a following with the right kind of posts, if that were the audience the family were after. A few shirtless shots and…

No. She wasn't here to sell him as some kind of thirst trap. She'd done her research. She knew about his *work*. His past as a young football player leading his country to an international championship. That was the sort of thing that people could get excited about. Even her blood had pumped a bit harder and the room had got strangely warm when she'd looked at the photographs of that long ago win. But he hadn't really answered where that man had gone. Sure, everyone grew up. But a lot of people continued to celebrate their past achievements. Had he disappeared under the weight of his role? It was hard to tell. Though it was clear, the future of the royal family was this man in front of her. Still, one thing stood out to her…

'To date, the story hasn't been about you, though. It's been about your role within the royal family. People only see you as part of a whole. A cog in a wheel.'

Something about him changed with those words. She didn't know what it was, but it seemed as though the man in front of her had been wearing a mask, which had suddenly melted away. She caught a glimpse of something more. The glint in his eyes of a person excited by possibilities. Because that was the first thing that had struck her when this role had been suggested to her. The world needed to see the man, not just the prince in official photographs from the palace. Maybe he wanted that too…

Her mind began working at capturing him in a more casual way. Behind the scenes. She loved taking photographs on her phone of the unscripted moments in life. Not just shaking hands with some foreign dignitary but turning Prince Gabriel into the sort of person everyone would clamour to know. He'd been that once, in his late teens and early twenties. They just had to tap into it again.

Except she wasn't sure how. People often froze when she held up her phone to take a photograph. Put on fake smiles. She'd checked the Halrovian royal family's social media accounts and they were *all* formality and fake smiles. Which was why her aim was to ensure that people were comfortable enough not to care about her being around them. So she tried to blend into the background, not to stand out.

Lena wondered if the man in front of her did anything less than formal, ever. He looked as if he were born in a suit. Maybe she could get him to loosen up a bit? Except there were no maybes. Her whole future depended on it. If she wasn't successful here, what was left for her?

'What changes do you propose?'

Prince Gabriel's question brought her back to the here and now. Not a future that she hadn't yet secured.

'You need your own social media accounts, to showcase *yourself* in your role as Crown Prince, not as part of the royal family.'

He checked his watch. A slender gold timepiece with a leather band. Not so showy, but something that screamed elegance and restraint. Ancient money. He was going to wind things up, she was sure. Her heart pounded a sickening, panicked rhythm. What if he sent her on her way without this job? What then? The role back in Isolobello didn't pay enough to support her and her family as it was a junior position. She needed something *more*.

Lena took a deep breath and settled her thoughts. She'd never really been to an interview like this before. Jobs had come to her because people perceived she had a talent. Yet she believed that the universe had been kind to her, given her opportunities. This was one now. Time to try being a little bold again.

'Your upcoming trip to Lauritania. May I ask what the royal family's social media team have planned?'

She'd seen the press announcing the trip. It hadn't all been positive, for some strange reason.

'It seems you've already asked. However, I'm unable to answer your question.'

'It'd be a perfect opportunity to introduce *you*, sir. Whilst I don't know the itinerary, I'm sure there'll be opportunities to show your life a little less scripted.'

Prince Gabriel narrowed his eyes. 'Let me be frank. I spend my life doing what I'm able for my country. That's the role I was born into. My consistent hard work for Halrovia should speak for itself...'

Lena's stomach dropped. He was going to let her go. What would she do now? Was a marriage of convenience to a rich man who saw her as a trophy whilst she mouldered in some grand home, dying inside every day, all that was left to her? Or perhaps a life like her mother's, mistress to a man who looked after her but didn't love her enough to *be* with her? Only catching snippets of the person you loved, yet not having all of him because that was the deal you'd struck with the devil. Her hands twisted restlessly in her lap. She tried to hold them still. Her prospective employer's face told her nothing.

'Yet it appears that my hard work and dedication doesn't mean anything at all. That I need more.'

He shuffled through some papers on his desk, straightened them. Clasped his hands on the desktop. He needed more?

'He needs you...' That's what Cilla had said.

'I'll give you a chance, Ms Rosetti, *only* because you come highly recommended by Princess Priscilla. Come on my tour to Lauritania. See what you can do. You're on probation for two months.' He fixed her with a stern, frigid gaze. 'Impress me.'

CHAPTER TWO

IF GABRIEL HAD thought that having someone managing his image would be harmless at best and an irritation at worst, he was wrong. It had only been a week and Lena Rosetti was driving him to distraction. Even worse, he was certain his parents wanted to exile her to the dungeons and order her execution, even though those kinds of punishments hadn't been utilised in Halrovia for centuries.

'Perhaps we could try the photograph with your jacket removed, Your Highness?'

Gabe wanted to pinch his nose against an impending headache. 'Why?'

'It'll make the picture feel slightly less formal. Younger audience? It'd be even better if you could roll up the sleeves of your shirt. Maybe remove your tie?'

She'd have him totally undressed soon. Would she blush if he removed more clothes? He enjoyed it when tinges of pink flushed her cheeks. Though Gabe didn't know why those thoughts entered his mind or why they seemed so enticing. He shook his head.

'You can have my jacket. The cuffs and the tie stay put.'

He stood. Shrugged out of his suit jacket under her watchful gaze. Was he mistaken, or did her eyes widen a fraction as he did? Lena came towards him with her hand held out and he passed her the jacket. As he did, their fingers brushed. It was like grabbing a live wire, the shock of sensation. Did she notice the same thing? He flexed his fingers, yet she seemed unaffected, taking the jacket and hanging it in a cupboard on the opposite wall.

'I am not removing *my* coat,' his father said.

'N-no, Your Majesty. I—I wasn't planning to make that request.'

'And why am I holding this compendium?' his father asked.

They'd been in Gabe's office for only fifteen minutes, trying to get the perfect shot as the photograph for the first social media post under his own name. For something supposed to be unscripted, this seemed to take a lot of directing.

Lena had initially asked Gabriel, his mother and father to simply talk whilst taking photographs on her phone. No photographers, she'd said. She wanted candid. That had been a disaster. Now, she was trying something else. Flitting about the office in her dark suit and distractingly bright golden yellow blouse, she looked like an overly industrious, somewhat harried, bee.

'Your Majesty, my idea is that I'll photograph you handing it to His Highness whilst Her Majesty watches on. The folder of what could be important papers signifies you "passing the baton", so to speak, to His Highness.'

Gabe's father narrowed his eyes. 'I am *not* passing the baton. The baton will pass when I do. Or should I decide to abdicate, neither of which events are in our near future.'

Lena didn't hesitate, which was a marvel in itself because his father's icy tone would have sent Halrovian courtiers scurrying. She appeared blissfully impervious or danger-ously ignorant to her impending doom. The King treated the crown with deadly seriousness. In the past he'd expressed determination to be the longest-sitting monarch in Europe, if not the world. Not even Gabe would have suggested a photograph with Lena's intended implication.

'It's figurative, Your Majesty. Designed to show trust in His Highness.'

The King gripped the dark, official folder a little harder, cast a piercing glance at Gabe. The problem was, his par-ents had tried to keep everything under such tight control, kept so much hidden, that he wasn't sure that they did trust him. They'd never encouraged him to attend university. He'd suspected the reason was they hadn't believed he'd be suc-cessful in his studies, given his dyslexia. Wanting to avoid the inevitable questions should he fail, even though their formal excuse was that he could more easily learn how to be a good king from his father. He tried to ignore the sense that, in some ways, he was an impostor to the role of Crown Prince. But what were his years of training at his father's side, if *not* for the moment he'd finally take the throne?

Then there'd been an argument about him having an in-dividual social media account as Crown Prince, as Lena had suggested. Managed by someone else other than the King and Queen's press secretary, not under the royal family's exclusive banner. In response, he'd fought hard for control of his own image. It had never mattered before. Gabe hadn't cared much at all, but the more control the royal machine tried to impose on him, the more he pushed back. He'd won, as he was always going to. Yet his parents weren't happy about it.

'Symbolism is important to a royal family, Miss Rosetti,' his mother said. Dressed in ice blue, her voice as frigid as the colour she wore.

Lena smiled as if impervious to the chill descending on the room. 'Which is why I would never ask His Majesty to hand over the sovereign's sceptre or the crown itself.'

Gabe knew what she wasn't saying. A folder made a statement, without really saying anything at all. It was all smoke and mirrors.

His father dropped said folder to the desk with a thud, displacing some of the supposed *important papers*. 'I don't like it.'

Lena's smile faltered. Something inside him burned with an angry heat at the look on her face. As if she'd somehow failed when, in truth, she was only trying to do her job.

She checked her phone. 'It's ten. Perhaps we could have a break for a few moments and resume with a new idea.'

'A coffee would be appreciated,' Gabe said. Preferably Irish, with a substantial swig of whisky.

'Of course, sir.' He liked the way she said that. The lilt of her accent. Her voice soft like the brush of a warm summer breeze against bare skin. 'Your Majesties?'

His father shook his head. His mother declined as well. Lena went to a carafe on the sideboard. Poured a cup, added a dash of sugar to take the edge off just as Gabe liked it. Took a little biscuit in some silver tongs and placed it on the saucer then walked to his desk. Today she was in heels, and he was transfixed by the way they made her hips sway gently as she walked. Though why he was even thinking about how she moved or how the skirt of her dark suit hugged her figure so well, he didn't dwell upon.

She was an employee, not a paramour.

Lena reached his desk and smiled as she carefully lowered the cup. The liquid inside trembled as she did, the cup overfull. As she placed it down the coffee sloshed over into the saucer, drowning the biscuit and overflowing onto the polished desktop. Her eyes widened.

'Oh, my goodness, I'm so sorry.' The words were said with such speed they almost became one. 'I—I—'

'Lena, it's all right.' He looked through the drawers of his desk and found some unused paper napkins and began mopping up the coffee whilst she looked at his parents, him, then picked up the cup and fled the room before he could provide some reassurance.

'That woman...' his mother said in Halrovian, which would have been unforgivably rude if Lena had still been with them—of course, his mother was never known for being overly polite to those significantly under her on the social ladder, who she didn't think in some way worthy '...is a hazard to the orderly running of your office.'

Lena was certainly something. A hazard to his equilibrium, the way she flitted about. Yet he felt strangely duty-bound to defend her.

'She comes highly recommended. Your private secretary endorsed her credentials. As did Priscilla.'

'Talk about handing over sceptres and crowns.' His mother sniffed.

'She was only asking Father to hand me a folder.'

'What are these important documents I'm supposed to be passing to you?'

His father picked up the embossed navy blue compendium from the desktop, opened it. Flicked over the first page. Stared for a moment. Began to chuckle. Closed the folder and handed it to Gabe. 'Indeed, most important.'

Gabe opened it as his parents looked on. Turned the page as his father had. There was a copy of a newspaper article. A headline, a picture of their greatest nemesis, masquerading as an advisor and supporter. Father to the young woman Gabriel had thought of as his girlfriend. Who'd seen fit to threaten betrayal of Gabe's trust because she wasn't going to end up as his queen. Awarding this man the position of Advisor of State was the price his parents had paid for his daughter's silence all those years ago. Except someone had scribbled on the picture in black. The man now had cartoonish horns. Dripping fangs. Flies buzzing round his head. He'd been turned into a comic villain.

Gabe shut the folder and glanced up at his father, who still looked entertained. Even his mother had a sparkle of amusement in her eyes. And there behind them, standing at the door with a faint wash of colour on her cheeks, stood Lena. Phone in hand.

Watching the scene with a look of something like guilt written all over her face.

Prince Gabriel's gaze locked on her, cold and assessing. Something about it made her shiver, but the sensation wasn't in any way unpleasant. What was he thinking? That he didn't like having his photograph taken without him knowing? Or had he seen her handiwork in the folder?

Nope, surely not. There was no need for him to look inside and when she'd snapped the winning picture the folder had been closed and everyone had been…amused. Maybe they'd been laughing about her. That his employee had all the grace and agility of a giant panda.

Heat rushed to her cheeks at the mortification of that thought. Lena cursed her clumsiness at almost spilling coffee all over her employer in front of his parents. In her defence, the King and Queen weren't an easy audience. She'd challenge anyone not to be a bumbling bundle of nerves around them, and she was *used* to royalty, given her past job. She'd despaired of getting the photograph she wanted. The one she'd imagined, an unscripted moment between monarchs and heir. If only she'd recognised earlier that all she'd needed to do was to leave the room to get the shot, it would have saved them time and a spilled drink.

Something about the realisation stung, that the only way Prince Gabriel might feel comfortable was if she wasn't there, but she was sensible enough to know that trust took time. Anyhow, she managed to get the shot she'd been looking for. The King chuckling at something and handing the folder to Gabriel. With the Queen standing on looking benevolent. It was the perfect moment. Looking warm and genuine even though the emotional temperature in the room had been about as balmy as the snowy peaks of the Alps in the distance.

'I think I have a photograph,' she said, lifting her phone and wiggling it as she came back into the room. As she approached Prince Gabriel's desk, Lena thought she heard his father mutter something that could have been *Thank God*, although she wasn't one hundred per cent certain. The King and Queen turned in unison to face her with the same assessing gaze as their son. Right now, with the three of them watching her with their matching icy blue eyes, it was rather like being trapped in a blizzard. Did she stay? Did she go? She decided to address the matter directly.

'Thank you for your time, Your Majesties. If there's anything you'd like to talk to His Highness about in private I can...' The looks the King and Queen gave her in that moment took Lena right back to her school days, when she was disdained by everyone for pretending not to know who her father was. It had stolen her confidence. Her voice. Instead of words, Lena pointed to the empty door and made walking movements with her fingers through the air. The King raised his eyebrows. The Queen watched on, stony.

'We're finished here,' Gabriel said. 'I'm sure Their Majesties have plenty to do today.'

Lena nodded. Curtseyed as his parents swept from the room without acknowledging her again.

After they'd left, her employer cocked an eyebrow. Then he lifted his hand and crooked his finger at her. 'Come here, Ms Rosetti. Sit.'

There was no question of not obeying his command. Something about the way his voice was so purposeful and stern caused another shiver to skitter over her skin, goosebumps following in its wake. Once again, the whole feeling more...needy than unpleasant. Lena moved across the thickly carpeted floor. Lowered herself into the chair opposite him. What was he going to do? The King hadn't looked upset, exactly. On the contrary, something had clearly amused him whilst she'd been dealing with the swimming saucer of coffee and drowned biscuit in the bathroom outside. Was His Royal Highness going to ask her to leave before she'd even really started this job? Her mother had always complained that she needed to comport herself better, that she was too free with her actions, didn't think about her words.

That she was too much.

So, she'd learned how to be *just enough*. But what was it about working in the Halrovian palace for their Crown Prince that made her hot under the collar? Her skin itch and prickle? As if she was *always* going to mess up, to do something wrong?

Gabriel opened the folder in front of him, and her heart froze, then dropped like an apple falling from a tree, right to her toes. He turned the page of the planner she'd begun putting together for social medial posts, to newspaper articles she'd printed, trying to get a feel for what was really going on in Halrovia. It had been difficult since she wasn't as fluent in the language as she would have wanted. Except, she'd doodled all over the picture of the man the piece featured because she hadn't liked the look of him...

Prince Gabriel took the sheet of paper out and held it up, facing her.

'Your handiwork?'

She swallowed, her mouth suddenly too dry. What could she do other than admit the obvious truth? She nodded.

'Why?'

Because the man in the picture had seemed...superior, but in a way that said he was looking down at you. Especially a person like her. One who'd come from a family with a single mother, even though it was the twenty-first century and who cared about that sort of thing any more? But she could never admit it, not to someone like a *prince*.

'I—I was just doodling. Is he a friend of yours?'

Gabriel gave what some people might have said was a

chuckle, but it had a sharp, dark edge to it. Not a happy sound. He looked at the paper and back at her. 'No. He is *no* friend of the royal family's.'

Relief flooded over her that she hadn't made yet another faux pas. 'He does have the appearance of someone who likes to sit in judgement of everybody.'

'You have experience of that type of person?'

To be honest, the King and Queen of Halrovia seemed like that sort of people, but that was just another thing in a long list she couldn't say, so she told another truth instead. 'A few headmasters and mistresses I've known.'

'Ah, hence the horns and fangs.'

He said it in a chilly kind of way but with the slightest upturn of his lips, suggesting that he found her scribbles amusing, but perhaps childish.

'I'm rather proud of those. I thought the flies about his head a nice touch.'

The corners of Prince Gabriel's mouth seemed to kick up a little more, threatening a real smile this time. Her heart thumped in heady anticipation, but the smile never broke free. 'They're quite masterful. Were you a keen student, Ms Rosetti?'

Lena stilled, trying to forget the memories that assailed her. She'd been miserable at school, but she'd always known that to have a future where she stood on her own two feet, she had to do well. To excel. So she had.

But she'd also wanted to make her father *notice* her. Hoping that if she achieved good marks, he might get to know her rather than remaining a distant figure whose feelings on anything she only really heard about through her mother.

'Your father is very proud of your results. He thought the card you made for him was touching.'

Yet he never delivered those sentiments to her personally. Sure, he'd been around, when he came to the home and for a few hours they pretended to play happy families. Yet Lena always had the sense that he looked at her and her brother more as though they were perfect specimens under glass, rather than real living and breathing children. And one day she'd opened her mother's bedside drawer and found the cards down at the bottom, as if her father hadn't cared enough to take them with him. Whatever he and her mother had shared, he hadn't shared any similar affection with her or her brother. He'd provided their genetic material. She guessed from what her mother had said that he'd applauded their achievements, but he hadn't cared to truly know them.

Those memories of that time ached deep inside. Not sharp any more, but now she was an adult she didn't understand having children if you didn't have some interest in them. Was her and her brother's existence all ego? She looked up at Gabriel, his frigid blue eyes once again pinning her to the spot. There were no answers there. She'd didn't know what it was about him. The cool, impassive kind of gaze. Not giving anything much away, piercing right through her.

Lena shrugged. 'I wouldn't say keen. I believe I succeeded to spite them. And you?'

Gabriel's eyebrows shot up. Why did she ask that? This wasn't some chit-chat over coffee, this was her employer. A *prince*. The things she could learn about him came from the Internet, or years of working with a person. Not this situation where she was a week into her job, finding her way.

Trying to figure out as much as she could about the rhythm and feel of the palace from other staff. His efficient private secretary. His secretive valet, who she'd bumped into in a private corridor of the staff quarters in the palace, where she thankfully had a small apartment as part of her role.

'I tried to do what was expected of me.'

It was an unusual kind of response. His school days didn't feature much at all in her online research, other than he'd studied at a prestigious Halrovian private school. She'd thought it strange that with all his advantages he hadn't attended university, announcing that his greatest education was to serve his people and learn beside the King. That had come surprisingly soon after he and his team had won the junior world football championship. He'd come home a hero. The small country in Europe overwhelming the giants of the game. It had been a triumphant moment. Lena wondered what made a young man give that all away.

'Was winning the junior world championship expected of you?'

Something about Prince Gabriel's gaze shuttered. She'd thought him closed off before, but she hadn't realised till this moment how much he showed if you cared to look hard enough. Right now, it was like a door slamming in her face. She immediately regretted her words.

'Winning was something I expected of myself, and for my team,' he said.

She wondered about the pressures of a prince and heir to the throne of his country. Working for the Isolobello royals, she hadn't much thought about it. Her royal family was loved, and their Prince had acquitted himself admirably when the King had fallen ill, guiding the country till his father's recovery. Then with Princess Priscilla, and the up-coming royal wedding, the whole country was entering the fervour of anticipated celebration, even though the wedding was still months away.

'Of course, but—'

'Those things are in the past. This is the present and where my focus lies. As should yours.'

She wanted to say that the past was what made him the man he was today, and that would help her shape the vision for his future. She didn't. Lena knew enough to stay quiet. She wasn't about to enter a full-scale argument with her employer when she was still on probation.

'Yes, sir.'

He stiffened a fraction, in almost a flinch. Then it was as if his body relaxed again. Like he was on familiar ground once more.

'You said you had a photograph?'

She nodded. She had a few to choose from on the phone they'd given her for work purposes. Luckily, none showing her offending doodling.

'Show me.'

She pulled up the album, picked the best picture and handed her mobile to him. His long fingers gently swiped the screen as he looked through. Stopping. The merest of frowns creasing his brow.

He handed the phone back. It was warm. A strange kind of thrill shimmied through her at the thought its heat came from his touch.

'What do you think?' she asked, before she could shove the words back in. Lena didn't know why it was impor-tant, but she wanted him to like the photo she'd taken. The warmth on his face like a balmy spring day. The moment she'd glimpsed the royals as real people, and not merely the embodiment of the position they held.

'It's the picture you described you wanted.'

'And are you happy for me to post it?'

'That's your job. What I'm paying you for.'

'But as you said before, it's your image. I want to know you're satisfied with what I've captured.'

He cocked his head a fraction, as if studying her. Then the corner of his mouth curled into the merest of sly, almost wicked smiles, which did all kinds of complicated things to Lena's insides that she didn't care to dwell on.

'I enjoy knowing that a successful picture meant to depict confidence and trust in the future of the monarchy was taken at the expense of a particularly irritating advisor of state whose ideas on the future of Halrovia don't always align with my own.'

Oh, she liked that a little too much. His hint of pettiness indicating that this man could be human with all the messy frailties that went along with it. That he wasn't so proper after all. *This* was a person who might be interesting to show. Something she would love to dive into and explore.

'What do you know of what's been happening here in Halrovia?' Gabriel asked, his question loaded with unspoken tension.

Lena knew a lot, having researched him, the family, and the situation. But there was an undercurrent she couldn't quite place.

'I know Princess Priscilla's getting married soon. And Princess Anastacia's already married...' After a reported whirlwind romance and engagement on the back of what appeared to be some unfair negative press, which seemed to have stopped after her wedding. Lena hesitated, some things falling into place now she really thought about them. 'It was around the time of Princess Priscilla's engagement that things changed, wasn't it?'

'She was never meant to marry Caspar. Anastacia was. But then love intervened.'

Gabriel almost spat out the word 'love', as if it were something unpleasant.

'Then Anastacia was involved in an accident, injured, and somehow the narrative began to turn against my family. We suspect that this man—' he tapped the clipping with her doodling '—is the instigator.'

Lena frowned. 'But you said he's an advisor of state?'

Gabriel nodded, quick and sharp. 'And yet, when it comes to power, people will do anything to get more of it. The ideas being promoted in the press aren't kind to my country—they're about self-aggrandisement and filling personal coffers. Yet he still gets to drive the narrative.'

Gabriel reached over to the corner of his desk where a newspaper sat folded. Opened it out, facing her.

'Read what it says.'

She wondered why he didn't read the headline himself, but didn't say so. *'"Is the Crown Worth the Cost? Critics Question Relevance of Prince Gabriel's Overseas Mission."'*

His eyes narrowed. 'Each day, this is what we're facing. It's insidious, and it's not the truth. My trip to Lauritania is about increasing trade and co-operation with a valued ally. That's good for the economy.'

She began to understand the royal family's problem. How

none of this was fair. Even more, she recognised the extent of the work she had to do. Especially when there wasn't an equal playing field between the truth before her and lies being told elsewhere.

'As for your "doodling",' Gabriel said, taking the offending paper between his fingers, 'I can't have anything that will cause an internal incident coming from my office.'

He stood and turned his back to her, his shoulders broad and strong. Enough to hold up the weight of his job, the weight of an entire country's needs. Then Prince Gabriel dropped the paper into a machine behind his desk. It buzzed, shredding the document.

'A few scribbles would cause a problem?'

'I'm not willing to take the chance. It seems everyone wants a piece of my family. Our special advisor is a man with an agenda. There's a small but strange push for a republic. Criticism now, where there was none before. It doesn't feel organic or authentic.'

'And if your people wanted a republic?'

Prince Gabriel sat behind his desk again, hands clasped on the gleaming wooden tabletop. 'Then they could have it.'

Lena gave a shaky kind of laugh. Surely he couldn't mean it?

'What? Give up? Just like that?'

'If I were King, my duty would be to honour and defend my people. If they didn't want my family ruling them and I couldn't convince them otherwise, then it would be my duty to stand aside.'

The way he said those words, with such strength and conviction, told her what he really thought. There was so much at stake here. If she failed… Then she'd be potentially responsible for the downfall of this man sitting in front of her, of a royal family. Lena wondered if her own shoulders were strong enough to carry the weight of her personal role here.

'But you don't want to. Stand aside, I mean.'

Gabriel shook his head. 'I'll never capitulate to this… propaganda. My family, me, *we* are the best choice.'

The morning sun streamed through the windows behind Prince Gabriel. He was lit up, magical and golden. How could anyone doubt he was the perfect prince? The king in waiting, who loved his country and would even set aside his own interests if his people wanted him to. Put a gleaming crown on his head and she could see it all laid out before her. Lena's heart quickened with excitement. She had no doubt. Gabriel Montroy *was* Halrovia's glorious future.

She just had to figure out how to show it.

CHAPTER THREE

LENA SAT AT an outdoor dining setting on a terrace, sipping a deliciously hot coffee as she overlooked the still, deep ink-blot of Lake Morenberg in front of her. The snow-capped Alps soaring behind, white peaks gleaming in the early morning sunshine. They'd arrived in Lauritania's capital the night before and she hadn't had a real chance to admire the beauty of the landscape until now. The home they were staying in was one of King Rafe's former private residences. An elegant, secure modern masterpiece with expanses of glass overlooking the water on one side of the house and, on the other, views into the old town and towering Moren-berg Palace they'd be visiting today.

She felt as though she'd had a kind of breakthrough with Prince Gabriel, small though it was. Their discussion over the real reasons why she'd been hired had given her more to work with. She liked to think it was some evidence of a growing trust that he'd disclosed those things to her, sensitive as they were. Giving her an insight into the true importance of her role. The challenge.

And that gave her ideas…

'Good morning, Lena.'

She startled at the deep, low voice of her employer behind her. Almost spilling her drink all over herself. She placed the mug carefully on the table and stood to curtsey and address him properly. As she did, he waved her away.

'Please. No formality, not here.'

He might have suggested no formality but even this morning he was dressed in suit trousers and a blue and white striped business shirt, which made his eyes seem even brighter. Though his hair was still slightly damp from a shower. Lena didn't know why that realisation ignited something warm in her belly.

It was likely just the coffee. She'd make a cooler cup next time.

'You talk about no formality yet here you are looking way too formal for this early in the morning.'

He took a long swig from the cup he held. 'I had a video call.'

'It's very rude of someone to organise something so early, before caffeination,' Lena said, sitting and taking another sip of her own delicious beverage.

'It was with my father.'

Lena choked, almost spitting out the mouthful. She coughed a few times, her eyes watering. 'My apologies, to His Majesty.'

'He's not here to see you, and…' Gabriel tapped the side of his nose, looking amused '…I'll never tell.'

She liked that. Someone seeing fit to protect her when no one really had. Gabriel stood for a few more seconds, staring out at the view as if lost in his own thoughts. A light breeze drifted over the terrace. She caught a scent on that breeze. Something so enticing that she wanted to simply breathe in a lungful. His aftershave, she guessed. Green, fresh, sweet, like she supposed the high alpine regions smelled. Coming from sea level and an island, she wasn't sure. Then he pulled out a chair from the table and sat down. Not *exactly* at the table itself, almost as though he was holding himself a little apart, when what he should be doing was trying to get closer to people.

Maybe he was an introvert and didn't really want to be around too many people. If that was the case, there were more ways to communicate with the world than by speaking. And after the seeming thaw between them, Lena thought it was as good a time as any to raise it. To push a little.

'Whilst I have you here…'

Gabriel cocked an eyebrow. 'Am I suitably caffeinated for this conversation?'

'I'll leave that for you to decide. I've been thinking, and I have some ideas about engaging with younger people.'

His face was devoid of expression apart from that perfectly cocked eyebrow. It remained.

'Please, enlighten me.'

Lena flicked through her phone. Pulled up a vision board she'd created. 'You're always in dark suits.'

'There's a problem with that?'

From her personal perspective, there was no problem at all. He looked impossibly handsome. Frankly, he could wear suits every day as far as she was concerned, and she could die a happy woman. Though why she was thinking like that she couldn't really tell. But she wouldn't be doing her job if she didn't suggest alternatives.

'In the right circumstances, no.'

'There's rarely a wrong circumstance in my role.'

It was as if this man didn't do anything that was fun any more. At. All.

'What about if you were…? I don't know. Judging a pet show at a local fair? With children bringing their favourite pet. And you had to pick the best one. Would a suit be right then?'

His eyes narrowed. He gave the slightest shake of his head. 'There is *never* a time I'd be doing that.'

'Well, maybe you should start. Everyone loves kittens and puppies, together with children. Totally relatable.'

'And what if a child's pet is something other than a kitten or a puppy? A snake, for example. Or a tarantula. I don't want to appear in any way relatable around those animals. I'd then wish to appear repellent.'

The sun had risen a bit higher in the sky, their little table now bathed in soft early sunlight. Lena's cheeks heated. She wasn't sure whether it was from the warmth of the sun or Prince's Gabriel's resistance to what seemed perfectly reasonable to her.

'See, Your Highness, now I think you're engaging in hyperbole.'

'There's a rule, *never work with children or animals*, for a good reason.'

'You're going to be King. If you rule out children and animals you're kind of forsaking some of the best bits of your "role", as you put it.'

'I'm not forsaking them at all, they simply haven't been in my repertoire. On the other hand, my sisters—'

'Are no longer available.'

He took a slow, and what sounded like a long-suffering, breath. 'You have a point to this conversation, I assume?'

'You're the one who took us offside with the talk of snakes and spiders.'

'And now I'm guiding us right back onside. Please get on with it. I have another meeting in fifteen minutes.'

'That's what I'm trying to do. I think you should try for a look that injects a little more colour. Something more casual. To mix things up a bit. Take a look.'

She handed over her phone to show him some of the pictures she'd found whilst trawling popular menswear blogs and social media for the latest looks. Before she'd started, she'd had no idea how much there was to learn about suits, and don't get her started on collar gaps. She had trouble looking at her employer now without analysing and admiring his impeccable tailoring. The way he moved, and the way his clothes moved with him…

'This—this—' He waved his hand over the phone as if it in some way offended him, which didn't bode well. 'No.'

Okay, so maybe some of the examples were a little out there, but she did get them from a viral men's fashion and workwear blogger who seemed to have real street cred.

'I'm just trying to show you that even if you're wearing a suit you can mix it up a bit.'

'The suit is mustard. The coat appears…shaggy.'

'But the look's stylish, even with all the colour, and shagginess as you put it. Which isn't really shaggy. It's mohair. And extremely expensive.'

He reached out and put his half-empty coffee cup down on the tabletop with a little bit too solid a thump. 'Cost *does not* equal taste.'

'But colour. A little more casual. All I'm trying to show you is that you can still look extremely stylish and…and…

princely. I'm sure that your valet would be able to sort something out.'

'Pieter would resign if he thought I'd wear this. Or call a doctor to see if I was coming down with something.'

'But you can't wear suits all the time. What do you wear when you're not working? When you're in your apartments just being…you? When you're…off the clock?'

His whole demeanour rankled. Sure, she needed the job, but she was also overwhelmed with the need to keep pushing, to get a hint of who he really was. And all she could hear was a voice in her ear from her mother that a woman should be an oasis. Still and deep. Welcoming. Somewhere that encouraged a man to *stay*. Even though her mother had been calm and cool like an oasis, her father had never stayed for long. Always going back to his real family.

Being an oasis was clearly not all that it was cracked up to be.

His Highness's eyes narrowed and once again she had the uncomfortable sensation of being skewered.

'I am never "off the clock", as you put it. I'm always available to help run the country. As for the rest, that's walking into personal territory you do not have permission to tread.'

'I understand, but you gave me a job. On probation if you recall. I want to make it something permanent. But I can only do that if you work with me a bit, or at least tell me what's off-limits.'

'I'll ensure you have a list of off-limits topics by later this morning, so you can study it at leisure.'

He looked at his watch and Lena sensed that he wanted to go. Her and her darned mouth. She needed to stop arguing with the man and regroup. 'I'm guessing that's all to be said on that topic, Your Highness?'

'Yes. You're free to leave.'

So, she was being dismissed. Back to square one, then. She stood and curtseyed even though he'd told her not to, then turned and began to walk towards the door leading back inside.

'Ms Rosetti?'

She turned and her breath snagged right in her throat. Once again, he was lit up by the sunshine that seemed to love him so much.

'Sir?'

'You haven't impressed me yet.'

Whilst Gabriel understood there was a certain amount of pomp and ceremony surrounding his role as prince, there was something about today that felt off. The meeting with his father had disturbed his usual early morning routine. Even worse was the King's attempt at giving advice, which was unwanted and unneeded. A fact that Gabriel had made very plain. Still, it was as if part of him didn't slot into place. He sat in the back of a large dark-coloured car with fluttering flags travelling behind a police escort. Usually, strangers believed he wanted to travel alone. However, he saw it as wasteful in both time and resources to have a procession of vehicles, one carrying him and the other carrying staff. He liked to spend the journey to any function preparing with his team. Talking, strategising. Yet today was a private function at the palace with Lauritania's King and Queen. The only person he had travelling with him was Lena. To take more photographs.

Perhaps that was what felt off. In this enclosed space with someone still unfamiliar, whereas his other staff had been with him for years. She hadn't spoken much apart from pleasantries, especially not after their conversation earlier about his clothes, where, if he was honest with himself, he might have been a little unfair.

Still, looking at Lena now, he thought she could hardly profess to be expert in all things casual and appealing to 'younger people'. Today she was dressed in a conservative black dress. High neck, skirt below the knee. It could have looked like a nun's habit except for the three-quarter sleeves showing her golden skin, and the way the dress seemed to perfectly shape to her body. Her hair in a bun that attempted to look tidy. However, dark stray hairs fell out of it, framing her face. Making her look soft, approachable. She wasn't paying attention to him, looking down at her phone, intent. For the first time in his life, he was at a loss on what to say. He simply watched her, nibbling on her lower lip as though she was concentrating.

As if she knew his gaze was on her, Lena blew away an errant strand of hair and looked up at him.

'I've been thinking,' she said. That didn't bode well. She'd been thinking when she suggested changes to his wardrobe as well.

'Indeed.'

'Have you ever considered having a meeting with business leaders in a more casual environment?'

Most of the time those kinds of meetings took place in a stultifying boardroom somewhere with PowerPoint presentations that flicked across the screen too fast for him to take in, and poisonously bad coffee.

'You have something else in mind?'

'I've heard you've been trying to fit in a meeting with the international youth mental health forum whilst you're here. I know you go for a run early, before breakfast—'

'How do you know that?'

He hadn't provided her with his early morning routine. It wasn't something he considered necessary. Gabriel didn't understand why he rather liked her knowing what he did so much.

'Pieter told me.'

Now *that* was a surprise. Pieter was a closed book. Not even the King and Queen could get information from him. It was always polite obfuscation. However, Pieter was also an excellent judge of character...

'When did you ask him?'

Lena tugged at the back of her bun as if adjusting the pins. 'This morning, before we left. I thought you could have a running meeting. It's early enough that people should be available. Plus, it fits because of the benefits exercise has on mental health. Afterwards you could offer everyone a free breakfast, if you wanted to.'

'And you get a photo of me looking casual...' She was clever. A simple suggestion that didn't sound manipulative at all, except he realised when he was being manoeuvred. 'What's to say I don't run in a suit?'

She snorted. 'Because that would be ridiculous, and you aren't in any way ridiculous. Plus, Pieter would never forgive you for doing that to one of your precious suits.'

Gabe couldn't help himself. He laughed. Lena's cheeks flushed a deep shade of crimson. Such a beautiful colour on her. He wondered what her plush, full lips would look like painted the same tone, rather than a neutral gloss.

'I'll see if it can be arranged.'

'I might have already raised it with your efficient private secretary.'

'Stop managing me, Ms Rosetti,' he said with a smile. Though he couldn't be angry about it. He relied on his staff being proactive. Anticipating his wishes and acting on them.

'I wouldn't dream of doing so, Your Highness.'

She had a sneaky, self-satisfied grin on her face. As if she enjoyed her little win.

'What's on the agenda today, to make me look good?'

He couldn't miss the rapid sound of her inhale. 'I think you're already looking quite…you know…'

She waved her hand about in his general direction. Did Lena think he looked good? That thought left him as satisfied as a cat given a bowl of cream. He shouldn't tease but he couldn't help himself.

'I'm not sure I do know. Please enlighten me.'

'Yes, well…you look very princely. Exactly like the description on the box.' Lena nibbled on her lower lip, the slash of pink on her cheeks darkening even further. She was terrible at trying to hide what she thought, or her own embarrassment. He decided to be kind. Change the subject.

'How was your first picture received?'

Lena blew out a long, slow breath, something like relief. 'Very well.'

'By whom?'

'The public. In the main.'

'Press?'

Since he'd been running late this morning, something entirely uncharacteristic for him, Gabriel hadn't had the time to get Pieter to fill him in on the usual news reports before work. To be fair, Pieter had told him that Lena was up and about extremely early and Gabe had wanted to give her space without her employer around. People always switched to work mode in his presence. That was all. No other reason, such as this strange sense of challenge he seemed to experience around her and enjoyed so much, rather than everyone's usual deference. Though he guessed challenging the palace status quo was what he'd hired her for.

Lena pulled up something on her phone, turned it to him.

He could catch some of the words, but he was still feeling…discombobulated. Out of sorts.

'I haven't got my glasses. Tell me what it says.'

Her eyebrows rose on her forehead. 'I didn't know you wore glasses.'

He didn't. His were a handy prop, which he put on occasionally enough to give himself the excuse that he didn't have them, should someone ask him to read something quickly. He just hadn't worn them recently. Still, Gabe didn't like to lie. For some reason, the sensation of discomfort over his untruth was especially acute with her. In the end, he shrugged.

Lena didn't question his silence. She turned back to her phone screen.

'"*Father and Son Moment: King's Support Shines in Prince's Online Breakthrough.*"'

'That's what you wanted, wasn't it?'

'It feels condescending to me. Honestly, as if you needed permission to open your own social media account. It's ridiculous.'

Something about her defence of him ignited a flicker of heat, deep inside.

'Anyhow, I prefer this one. *"Prince's Social Media Debut: Millions Follow as King Hands Over the Reins."* Though I'm guessing His Majesty will never forgive me.'

Both parts of what she'd said gave him pause to reflect, but he dealt with the one where a sound of uncertainty had infiltrated her voice.

'His Majesty has no influence here. I protect my loyal staff.'

She smiled, and it was like the sun peeping out from behind a cloud. Bright and warming for a fleeting moment, then it was gone.

'Thank you,' she said.

'As for the rest, you said…*millions*?'

Gabe hated the way that he sounded even mildly interested or surprised, when he'd never cared before.

'Millions, within the first few hours. Seems you're more popular than anyone knew.'

'There are those who disagree.'

'I'm not one of them.'

Somehow the inside of the vehicle's temperature seemed to rise, even though it was air-conditioned. Gabe adjusted his tie a fraction.

'There's much about the narrative that's unfair. My sister Anastacia, for example. She was always thought of as the Perfect Princess. Then she had an accident. It…' Crushed her. How she'd been treated as if she'd been in some way damaged by her scarring. Even by his mother. 'It…affected her. She hid away whilst recovering. Hid her scars. Some in the press accused her of being work-shy.'

'People are cruel. The tabloids especially. But now she's married, and the press seems favourable again. Then they turned their attention to you.'

Lena's voice was quiet, sombre. As though she'd had personal experience of cruelty, which he wanted to explore. However, it wasn't his place.

'So it seems,' he said.

The car turned off onto the short but winding road that took them to Lauritania's palace. Yet somehow, he didn't want this journey to end.

'I'll do what I can to stop it.'

Lena shifted her hand, almost as if she was reaching out to touch without thinking. He held his breath for the moment her skin met his, but it never came. She drew her hand back instead. A sense of heaviness weighed down on him. Why did he crave that touch so much? He couldn't understand. Perhaps it was that his family had been in crisis-management mode for what felt like so long, he hadn't been touched recently. There hadn't been the time or the inclination. Perhaps he *should* clear a space in his diary for a night or two of adult enjoyment. Except that didn't seem to hold any interest either.

Nothing much did.

The car slowed, pulling up to a private entrance at the palace. A member of staff opened the door and Gabe exited whilst Lena followed him into the building, her footsteps clicking on the marble floor behind him. Today he was meeting his godson for the first time since his christening, delivering a birthday present for what Lena had said would be a noteworthy moment, and something that would allow him to show a softer side.

They were ushered through an oak door to the King and Queen's private quarters. As he saw them, he bowed. Unnecessary amongst friends, perhaps. But Lena was here.

Lauritania and Halrovia were close allies, and that had survived the death of most of the Lauritanian royal family in a tragic accident. Leaving their Princess, who had never been expected to rise to the throne, as Queen. Annalise and her husband, Rafe, were beloved. He could only wish for the same for himself and whoever might be his queen one day. Gabriel caught a glimpse of Lena in his peripheral vision, carrying his birthday gift for the little prince and something for his sister too, so the little girl wouldn't be jealous. That had been Lena's own insightful suggestion. Gabriel was struck by how impressive a woman she was. To garner Priscilla's confidence, Pieter's apparent trust. Managing his parents… *Him.*

'Gabriel.'

Queen Annalise reached out, giving him a warm embrace. He shook hands with Rafe. Exchanging the normal pleasantries, although he understood it was somewhat more stilted than usual with Lena in the room, since they didn't know her.

'Your Majesties, I'd like to introduce Ms Lena Rosetti,' he said as Lena curtseyed, 'who's in charge of my… PR.'

Lise smiled at Lena, always gracious. 'Welcome! Goodness, a PR manager. How long have you been with His Highness?'

'Around two weeks, Your Majesty.'

'I hope it's going well. Is His Highness doing everything you ask of him?'

Lena gave an enigmatic smile. 'I couldn't say, Your Majesty.'

'How politic of you.' Lise laughed. 'I'm afraid we're rather old-fashioned here. Perhaps we need a PR manager too? If you're ever seeking different pastures, you might get in touch...'

Those words lit something volcanic inside Gabe. He instantly wanted to shout *No!* although he had no reason to. Whilst it had only been a couple of weeks, he'd begun to value Lena in ways he couldn't explain.

'I'd ask you not to try to steal my staff right in front of me,' he said.

'No, we'll do it behind your back like any decent prospective employer would,' Rafe said with a grin. He'd been a ruthless businessman before marrying Lise. The ruthlessness remained, at least where his wife and what she wanted came into play.

That thought left Gabe feeling strangely wistful, as if looking for something he didn't know was missing. He shook it off.

Gabe turned to Lena. She stood there looking professional, impassive, although her blue eyes glittered with glee as if she was enjoying the unofficial bidding war.

'If these...poachers approach you, let me know. I'll give you a pay rise.'

Lena cocked her eyebrow. 'Sir, I believe they have already approached me. So, I'll leave that with you.'

'She's ruthless, Montroy,' Rafe chuckled. 'I like her.'

Gabe had come to realise he did too. She was fresh. Honest. Didn't pander to him. He tried not to think about the rest. Like her colouring. So striking, with her hair as black as a raven's wing, eyes like blue topaz. Skin a burnished gold.

Lena made a transfixing picture, should you take the time to notice her.

'I'm supposing you'd like some photographs, then?' Lise asked, bringing his thoughts back to the real purpose of Lena's presence.

'Yes, ma'am. I understand, whilst these are part of your private apartments, you do occasionally use this room as a formal receiving area for international guests. Is that correct? I want to make sure your private space remains private.'

'You're correct.' Lise cocked her head, her gaze on Lena intense. Gabe wondered what she was thinking. Probably how much to pay Lena to tempt her away from him. Gabe made a mental note to take that quip about a pay rise seriously. 'Thank you for being so thoughtful.'

'I was also wondering, ma'am, whether we could take a photograph of His Highness with Prince Carl. From behind, not showing your son's face. I appreciate you're careful with your children's privacy.'

Lise and Rafe exchanged a glance. 'Of course. Why don't I bring them in now? I know they're looking forward to seeing you, Gabriel. Especially as you come bearing gifts.'

For his godson, he'd brought the present he always gave children for their birthday. A book. Because reading was the greatest gift Gabe could bestow. One he'd come to finally enjoy through audiobooks, and, if persistent, by slowly reading novels when he had the time and was in the right frame of mind. Something he could never have enjoyed when he was younger.

Queen Lise left the room and returned within minutes, two squealing children running behind her, the room filling with chaos and laughter. Once again, a sensation assailed him watching the scene. Rafe, hugging his little boy. The little Princess and future queen, showing her mother something she'd drawn. He'd only ever seen marriage and family as a duty to his country. From his pre-teens he'd been told that was his role, to assure the throne with the correct partner and at least two children. It had never held an attraction as anything other than another job, securing succession.

Yet, seeing the family tableau in front of him, why did he suddenly crave for something more?

Lena melted into the background. The King and Queen made a beautiful couple. The Queen with her golden colouring and Rafe with his dark good looks. The children mirrored their parents. The little Princess Marie a whirlwind of dark curls taking after her father, and the Prince, a golden cherub like his mother.

She tried to capture it all. Gabe had been right about not working with children or animals. She had a hard time getting any shots without the children's sweet faces but she was sure that their parents might appreciate some of the photographs for their own album, so she stopped worrying and simply took pictures.

The Princess loved the sparkly fairy costume with wings and a crown they'd brought so she wouldn't get jealous. She ran about bestowing favours and wishes to everybody with a tap of her wand. Lena had almost expected Gabe to be as cool and aloof as usual, but he wasn't. Not here. She'd come to realise that his chilly persona wasn't the real man. There was someone else entirely simmering underneath his impeccable suits. Lena was sure he was hiding part of himself. She just didn't know what, or why.

It was a puzzle to sort out at another time. Right now, he sat at a little child's table opposite his godson, who was colouring in a picture with crayons. It was such an incongruous scene. Such a large man in a suit, folded into a small chair opposite a child. She picked up the book he'd brought with him and walked towards them both.

'I know you've forgotten your glasses, sir. But perhaps you could show Prince Carl the pictures?' She spread open a page adorned with colourful animals on the table between them. Gabe looked up at her as she did. She couldn't fathom the expression on his face as she stood back. It almost looked guilty.

'Why don't you draw me a fish like this?' Gabe said, pointing at the page as Carl took a blue crayon and began to scribble on some paper. Lena stood behind him, photographing as Gabe turned the pages. It was such a tender scene. The two princes. With his blond hair, Carl could almost look like Gabe's son. In that moment, a gripping sense of the future overwhelmed her. Was this what he'd be like as a father? Someone attached, interested?

She'd never had that. In truth, she hadn't really wanted it until she'd gone to school and the other students had told her it was what their fathers were like. Lena had realised, after trying to engage with her own, that he was never going to be there for her. Yet what was she seeing here? If she'd had children, it was what she'd want for them. A father who wasn't distant and aloof, but who was proud of them and their achievements. Who wanted to spend time with his children doing something as simple as looking through a book. Praising their drawings.

It left her melancholy, with a sense that she'd missed out, even though she'd had a good enough life. Been given an education. Had a mother who loved her, in her own way. Always food on the table. That was more than many had. She should be thankful. Lena couldn't say why it left a bitter taste in her mouth.

'I think I have enough now,' she said. 'I've taken lovely pictures of the children that I believe Your Majesties would like, which I can send to you. Do you want to pre-approve any before I post them?'

'No,' Queen Annalise said. 'I trust your judgement.'

'Thank you, ma'am. I feel privileged that you do.' That was the truth. Like when they'd talked about offering her a job. Lena wasn't silly enough to think it was anything serious, although she had the sense there was more to it from King Rafe's perspective, at least. Otherwise, it was all just a bit of banter between people who were familiar with each other.

More than familiar. She looked around the room. These people were clearly friends. Lena had never really had the same. Her mother hadn't encouraged it for fear that Lena would want to reveal who her father was, or that they'd search for information about him. And if she had friends, she'd probably want to spend some time without an employee hanging about. 'I might take your leave and let you catch up.'

'It's almost morning tea. I'll ask my private secretary, Albert, to meet you outside and take you for refreshments.'

'Is there anything else, sir?'

She addressed her question to Gabriel, who looked up at her with an intensity that branded skin. 'That's all. Thank you, Lena.'

Lena curtseyed, then walked out of the room. Chased by the confusing feelings she was desperate to leave behind.

CHAPTER FOUR

GABE SUCKED IN the cool morning air as his run ended. It was just past six thirty and he'd been surprised at how successful Lena's suggestion had been. Many of the highest profile participants at various mental health charities had joined him. It was a slower run than normal, along the banks of the magnificent Lake Morenburg in Lauritania's capital. They'd jogged the paved paths around the lake, followed by security at a discreet distance and some press, taking the time to talk about youth mental health and strategies for improving it. He'd missed Lena this morning, her constant presence. After a few photographs at the beginning she'd gone back to the residence they were staying in. Waiting for their inevitable arrival for a breakfast that had been arranged to continue talks in a casual environment.

Gabe hoped to make a difference. Even with all his privileges, he had some knowledge of what despair felt like. When no one could understand why he fell behind at school. Not listening to him when he said something was wrong, believing it was lack of effort rather than a true inability. It was only when he began to find sport that he'd come into his own, recognising there was something he was good at and he wasn't a complete failure. His sports teacher had also listened, suspecting the dyslexia that had finally been diagnosed.

The group jogged up the winding private path to King Rafe's home outside the palace. A perfect place to escape. It wasn't the first time Gabe had stayed here, and it was always on offer for him should he want to get away. That didn't seem enough any more. Whilst living at the palace in his own wing back home was a convenience, his time on this trip had led him to conclude he needed more. A place of his own, not something owned by the family. As he climbed the stairs to a particularly beautiful terrace overlooking the lake, Gabe made up his mind. He'd set his private secretary on the path of locating a home to purchase for himself. Whilst he was going to be King one long-off day, he was tired of having others trying to control him. Striking out on his own hadn't seemed necessary before. Now, it was somehow vital. Gabe reached the top of the stairs, where the view was most breathtaking. He wanted a place like this, with privacy and solitude. One he could staff himself, make his own choices.

Lena.

Thoughts of her came to him unbidden. He'd arrived at the expansive, tiled terrace where she was waiting, as if for him alone. What a ridiculous thought. Of course she was waiting for him. He was her employer. She was there with his private secretary, to greet the guests, which she did with charm. Gracious as always, eliciting smiles. Yet this morning, she looked different, in a way that unbalanced him.

He'd only ever really seen her in muted colours. Blacks, dark blues, making it easy for her to melt into the background. She always looked striking. However, this was something else. Not a suit, but a dress in an ochre yellow, with white flowers and burgundy accents. The colour made her golden skin glow as if lit up by sunshine. But it wasn't simply the colour that attracted him. It was the style. The dress wrapped round her body. The skirt grazing her calves with a flirty frill. The fabric skimming her curves, her body. Silky and light, fluttering in the breeze. A gust blew, hitching the front of the skirt, flicking it back. Lena smoothed it down though he knew that another gust, a little stronger, might expose a hint of her thigh.

Gabe was transfixed, he couldn't take his eyes from her, trying to catch a mere glimpse of her skin like some errant teenager. He moved from her long, lithe legs but it was almost worse, his gaze snagging on the top, the way it settled between her breasts in a vee. Wrapped round her torso, tied at the waist in a bow.

He couldn't get out of his head that she was wrapped up as if some kind of gift, just for him. For his pleasure. What he wouldn't give to reach out, tug the bow at her waist. Undo her. Unravel them both.

It was impossible. He was a prince, with expectations to marry a princess. She was his employee. Yet all he could think of was the need coursing through him. A relentless drumbeat of desire.

Why her, out of all the women he'd spent time with? Lena turned, and looked at him, her lips the same burgundy as the flower details of her dress. Another gust and her ebony hair whipped about her face. He held his breath as the corner of the skirt flicked, and for a fleeting moment he caught it, a slice of smooth, golden thigh. A powerful spike of lust struck him. He craved to—

'Your Highness?'

Lena's words dragged him out of his reverie as she walked towards him. How hadn't he noticed the sway to her gait? How her hips moved in such a hypnotic kind of rhythm? What would the press say if they could see him now?

Proper prince indeed.

'Has it been a successful meeting so far?'

'Yes. Thank you for the excellent suggestion.'

A hint of pink feathered her cheeks. He'd come to relish that colour. It was a beautiful look on her.

'I thought I might mingle. Take more photographs.'

He noticed some other men in the group admiring her. He didn't know why he was possessed with the desire to hide her away from their gazes. It was ridiculous. She was a grown woman who could look after herself. There was no need for him to be her champion in some misplaced chivalry, and yet the clawing sensation remained. He ignored it. Yet he couldn't get over the sensation that if he didn't do *something*, she'd be stolen away from him, when he had no claim on her at all.

'Whatever you need to do.'

She nodded. Her attention already on others in the group, no doubt thinking of who to approach first. These were all high-profile members of the business community. Anyone here could see her competence and professionalism, like Lise and Rafe yesterday. She made to leave, walk away from him. He was overcome by the desire to make her stay.

'Lena.'

'Yes, sir?'

Say my name. It was unfeasible. Yet he didn't know why he so badly wanted to hear it. Like it was some inevitability.

'If anyone offers you employment, tell me. I was serious yesterday at the palace.'

Her eyes opened wide. 'I—I…of course. I wasn't planning on going anywhere. I've only just begun.'

He nodded as she walked to a group, and they shuffled together as she held up her phone. Smiled for her. He marvelled at her openness, how she brought out the best in people.

How, in many ways, he felt as though he'd only just begun, himself.

It was clear that the breakfast was a success. When Lena had mentioned the plan, Prince Gabriel's private secretary had immediately jumped on the idea. She liked that she could contribute in a way that was more than photographs and some words on a social media site. She was beginning to feel as if she was part of a little team.

She took some more pictures, trying to ignore the prickling of awareness of her employer's presence. She'd only ever seen him in a suit and he'd joked he might wear one running, yet today he was in workout gear. It was just a T-shirt, shorts, trainers. Yet she was drawn to keep looking at him. The way that T-shirt moulded his body. Showing his biceps. His broad shoulders. The shorts, not tight, but still framing his backside. The sheen of perspiration on his skin. Had she not been used to keeping a tight rein on her emotions she might have swooned. There was a reason he'd hit the 'hottest men in Europe' lists more than once, though they'd always noted how remote he seemed, which tended to be a factor running against him most of the time.

Right now, he topped every one of her personal lists. Professional, considerate, attentive, caring, handsome. *So* handsome. He laughed at something someone said, and all of him lit up. How could anyone call him cold? Surely others could see what she could? Yet she needed to stop looking. It had become like some obsession. Instead of constantly tracking him whilst he ate or talked to his guests, she checked media alerts on her phone.

Cold No More: Crown Prince Melts Hearts as He Bonds with Toddler Godson

The headlines looked positive. Talk of his diplomacy. Applauding him showing his softer side. She was particularly proud of her photograph. Gabe, with a soft expression on his face. A warm smile, pointing out things in the book. Carl, looking on, his back to the camera. His parents out of focus in the background, but you could still tell there was an indulgent kind of expression on their blurred faces.

A slide of warmth slipped through her veins. She was glad she'd been able to show how genuine it was, because it hadn't been an act, it had been real. Authentic. A tender moment that more people needed to see he was capable of.

She was tempted to look over at him once more, before this morning's event ended and he wrapped himself in the confines of a suit again. She guessed it was his uniform of sorts. His shield. His protection. Much like her sombre professional wardrobe, which she'd decided to cast away on a whim this morning because it was a beautiful day and…she really didn't know. She supposed it was because she wasn't out in public. She didn't have to stay in the background so as not to outshine her employer. Even so, she'd got a little thrill putting on the dress and had fleetingly wondered whether he'd liked it when he first saw her. Lena tried to ignore what

Gabe might think of her outfit, and instead concentrated on his social media pages.

She wished she could be analytical about it all, but she always got a bit of a buzz if something she posted did well. Underneath the photograph with him and his godson, there were so many comments.

This is the sweetest!

Such a gorgeous photo.

All reflecting the majority of the news headlines, apart from some of those in Halrovia, which still tried to put a negative spin on the post. Criticising the money spent only to show these 'homely' moments. She gritted her teeth at the unfairness of it, on Gabriel's behalf.

Lena grabbed a cup of coffee and took herself to a secluded part of the terrace in the shade and continued scrolling down. There were still a few people muttering about a republic but there weren't too many grinches today, because who couldn't help but love a picture of Gabriel being a doting godfather? The posts in response were emojis. Smiles, hearts. *Flames.* Glancing over at him standing there with his broad shoulders, narrow waist and strong thighs, she got it. She really did. Flames were apt. If the people who'd posted that could see what she saw right now, they'd want to fan themselves as much as she wanted to. They'd probably need a moment to catch their breath too, because it was as if she'd been on the run, not him, the way she couldn't catch any air.

Then there were the other posts that sent a spike of something hot and potent through her, which wasn't about attraction. If Gabriel were her boyfriend, she'd be sure the sensation was one of jealousy. It had to just be indignation on his behalf, because she didn't like being objectified, so why should he? Talk of ovaries exploding. Things like, *This picture made my heart melt, and my panties too*. Or, *Forget the book. Can I get a prince like you for my birthday?*

She tried not to judge. Who wouldn't want a prince for their birthday? Although she wasn't sure why she was thinking that, since she'd never wanted a prince before. She had no romanticism left in her, not after her parents. Still, the comments made her feel something prickly she couldn't explain, so she didn't try. She just kept reading. The sweet ones and the steamy. Unable to explain the roller coaster of her emotions as she viewed them.

'Lena.'

Gabe's voice jolted her out of her reverie. She whipped round, heel catching on the sandstone paving of the patio, hand jerking and an arc of coffee flying as Gabriel caught her, and they ended in a complicated tangle, with her somehow in his arms and him with a splat of coffee across his shirt.

He looked down at her for a heated heartbeat. Apart from the coffee she'd just spilled all over him, he smelled like the sea today, clean, salty, with an undertone. Something woodsy. It was complex. Inviting. A scent she wanted to snuggle into and stay, not moving from his strong embrace, with him looking down on her as if she could somehow answer the secrets of the universe...till she realised where she was. In her employer's arms, at an official function in front of a crowd of business people. She began to wriggle free.

'Are you all right, Ms Rosetti?'

His voice sounded somehow deeper, gravelly. Except she

couldn't help notice that he was back to being formal. Putting her in her place.

'Yes, of course. The heels. I shouldn't have worn them out here. Silly me. I'm as clumsy as a newborn donkey sometimes.' Her mother's taunt was useful right now.

'Have you ever seen a newborn donkey before?'

'Well, no…' What could she do? What could she say? Her heart pounded a sickening rhythm. She'd made a fool of herself, of him, in front of all his guests. Not at all demure. She tried to shut down her mother's voice 'But, Your Highness. Your shirt!'

She untangled herself from him, grabbed a bundle of napkins and began patting away at his chest. Trying to mop up the coffee ruining the fabric of his tee. Making it stick to what she could see were the impressive muscles underneath.

The heat roared into her cheeks.

'Ms Rosetti…'

Lena couldn't stop. She was desperate to clean up the mess she'd made. She kept patting, the white napkins staining with coffee, but it didn't seem to make a difference.

'Lena.' He put his hand over hers. She stopped, defeated, looking up at him. His pupils were huge and dark in the pale, icy blue of his eyes. Nostrils flaring. Lips parted. 'A new shirt is on its way.' She didn't know how, since she'd only just flung a coffee over him, but sure enough Pieter had arrived carrying a fresh shirt. Gabriel released her and took it from his efficient valet.

'I'm sorry,' she said, 'I—'

He held up his hand. She noticed how broad the palm was, how long and elegant the fingers. Remembered how it had felt when those hands had cradled her. Had she imagined how gentle he'd been? Yes, she must have. He didn't want her to fall, that was all.

'Accidents happen. Why don't you go and put on some safer shoes for this surface? When you return someone wants a photograph with me. They were meant to come to dinner at the ambassador's residence tonight and can't make it.'

He gave her a short sharp nod as he headed inside. She looked around her, but no one had seemed particularly bothered by her moment of clumsiness. It was only her, wanting to die inside from embarrassment, all the while unable to forget what it felt like to be in his arms.

This evening had been a long one. Gabriel strolled down the dimmed hallway of the Lauritanian home, trying to stay quiet as everyone appeared to be asleep. He understood there were people here who'd be at his beck and call should he so desire, but he didn't need anyone. Or perhaps he needed only one person.

A woman who was his employee. One who'd felt far too good in his arms when he'd held her this morning. In that glorious dress, showing off her feminine side. Lips like wine. The scent of her, delicious, as if she'd bathed in honey and chocolate.

If he'd been any other man he might have kept on holding her. Might have tried to kiss her, even though his sensible side told him that was impossible. Yet after a long evening, he'd begun to wonder why.

He needed to get her out of his head. However, he couldn't stop thinking about their conversations. What made her different? That slight irreverence for his position she tried to hide. The sense of freedom about her that led him to consider that life might not be as constrained as his family believed. Her defence of him, her seeming belief in him as a man, and as Crown Prince. In her insightful photographs of him, showing a side of himself he'd forgotten.

He liked it, far too much. Craved it. Which was why he hated lying to her about his reading. About his glasses. Did he trust her enough to disclose what the real problem was? Would she judge him for it, for not being truthful?

He couldn't be sure. His own staff didn't care. He'd adapted, and technology made things so much easier there was no need to tell anyone outside his immediate circle because it was irrelevant. Wasn't it? Right now, he didn't have a good answer to that question whereas once, he wouldn't have thought twice about it. Tonight, it was as if the world weighed him down. He'd been to dinner at the Halrovian ambassador's home—a routine event when visiting another country, to drop in on the person flying Halrovia's flag. It had been a tedious kind of evening, because he'd seen it for what it was: conversations about the state of Halrovia, the press's views on the royal family, and the ambassador giving his own advice, because he was a good friend of Gabriel's father.

But the hints had come thick and fast about the benefits to a population's mood from a royal wedding. As if it weren't enough that Cilla was to be married in a few months, and that Anastacia had married only a few months earlier herself—although that hadn't been a royal wedding. It was a private function at her fiancé's chateau. Whilst his parents might have looked down on the occasion because it didn't meet their lofty expectations, Gabriel found something about it to be strangely satisfying. She'd married a commoner, someone she was in love with. Someone who had made her deeply happy. It was all he could ever have asked for both of his sisters.

As for himself, he'd been quietly reminded tonight of where his duty lay and, for once, he wanted none of it. He'd begun to realise that Lena's success was vital, if nothing else to ensure that more pressure wasn't put on him to marry. It wasn't that he believed he couldn't withstand it. He was his own man and wouldn't succumb to the whims of others, but over the past couple of weeks something had made him question life as he knew it.

He had rounded the corner towards his room when the unmistakable light tap of footsteps behind him made him stop and turn.

'Your Highness…' came the soft voice. 'Sir.'

It was as if the weight pressing down on him had lifted. He'd only ever seen Lena polished and professional, yet tonight she was in jeans with a soft pink top covered in butterflies. Her hair slightly damp, as if she'd just come out of a shower. He refused to dwell on that thought, on how rivulets of water would look running over her golden skin…

'How was this evening's dinner?' she asked.

The truth didn't bear mentioning. He'd done his duty—been polite, chatting to the guests, and then leaving. It had been cordial, but a pointed reminder from his parents as to what they expected from him.

'Walk with me,' he said as he set off towards his room. To remove his suit. Wash away the evening of expectation like a taint from his skin.

'How are things back home?' she asked.

He was fully aware she'd be keeping a pulse on what was going on—that was part of her job—but small talk suited him right now as the anger churned in his gut. He was an adult, and yet he was still being served missives by his parents through intermediaries.

That lack of communication irked him. He realised tonight how often so much went unsaid in his family. At least with Lena, she said what she thought. There was no guessing. In the palace and with the courtiers it was all about subtle messages you had to unravel. Reading between the lines. He was tired of it. They arrived at his suite and Gabriel walked straight to the credenza and poured himself a whisky. He held up the glass.

'Would you like one?'

Lena shook her head and held up a mug.

'Hot chocolate's my choice.'

Was that why she'd smelled like chocolate so often? Of course, it'd be improper to ask. She placed her lips round the rim of the cup and took a sip. As she did, her eyes fluttered shut as if in pleasure. The hint of a chocolate scent teased his senses. That smell of rich sweetness. Would her lips taste as sweet if he kissed her?

He slammed the door shut on those imaginings.

'The ambassador thinks an effective strategy is for me to marry.'

Lena was mid-sip when he said the words. She stopped, pulling the cup from her mouth. 'Well, people do love weddings.'

'Do you think it would be an effective strategy?' he asked.

'Spending the rest of your life with someone isn't a strategy.' The words sounded bitter in her mouth.

'Do I detect some cynicism?' he asked.

'You tell me—you're the one who's talking about getting married to improve your popularity. I can't think of anything more cynical than that.'

He shut his eyes and pinched the bridge of his nose, the pressure in his head building, because he agreed. Gabe wondered why that expectation had never really bothered him before. He'd always understood his duty, it had just seemed so distant before.

'Anyhow, who is the ambassador to say something like that to you?'

Wasn't that an excellent question? 'He's a friend of my parents, and he'd invited some suitable candidates as well.'

'Did any take your fancy?' Lena asked.

He'd realised their purpose—a few who might tempt his eye as potential brides. Whilst his parents would expect a princess, the women present were still eminently suitable members of various aristocracies. Then there were a few others who might tempt him in a different way, should that be where his inclinations lay. Once again, beautiful, polished, interesting, and yet he had no interest in any of them.

'If they had, I'd still be there.'

Lena pursed her lips, displeasure written all over her face. 'Pardon me for speaking plainly, but I find the whole thing odd.'

He took another slug of alcohol, somehow enjoying how prickly she'd become.

'So do I,' he said.

'Then why subject yourself to it? How dare people tell you how to lead your life?'

She seemed all flash and fire and he didn't quite understand why in that moment the thought of him having to marry for his role, and not for love, seemed to anger her. It was the way it tended to be done in most royal families, though the pretence of choice was still there. Put two people who met the correct criteria together, point them in the right direction with some solid encouragement and they usually got the message. Although Cilla and Ana had seen fit to break the mould...

'You're *curating* my life.'

'That's different and you know it. I'm showing people a glimpse, giving them some good news. But I'm not faking. I'm just giving people the best of you. It's what everyone does.'

Yet he was faking it in many ways. He wondered again, how she'd feel if she knew about his reading difficulties. He could share it with her, right now. She'd signed a non-disclosure agreement but, even more, he was sure she'd never breach his confidence even without that formal document. He took another sip of his drink, priming himself. Yet he couldn't find the right words. Time enough for confessions later. Instead, Gabe focussed on something easier, the desire to know what Lena thought was the best of him. *That* seemed vital. He supposed he could look at his own social media account, but he never had before. The one piece of advice he took away from his brief interactions in that public space, and warnings from Cilla when she'd first suggested Lena for the role was, *never read the comments.*

It seemed like wise advice.

'So, how do you curate your own life?' he asked.

She took another sip of her drink. He joined her with his own.

'I don't have social media in my real name. And I don't post for myself. It feels too much like work. I tend to people-watch instead.'

Something about her was shuttered. Closed off. As though there were things she didn't want to talk about, and he was treading close to them. He was assailed by a grasping need to find out why, to throw all her doors open and to peer inside. Yet he had no rights to the information as her employer. But for a woman who was happy to lay people's lives bare online, he found it surprising she wanted to keep herself hidden.

'What about your work? Surely that's all about being online?'

'Word of mouth's important. I got my job with you because of your sister. No one wants the most important person in their story to be the employee who manages their PR and social media. My job is to stay in the background, make my employer look good. As for the rest? I'm unimportant in the general scheme of things.'

He didn't know why those words seemed wrong. Was that how she thought of herself? Or was it someone else putting those thoughts into her head? He knew too well how family could cut. His sisters, particularly Cilla, had borne the brunt of his mother's disapprobation. The public's too, for not fitting a mould cast for her. Then Ana, who the press had loved as Halrovia's *'Perfect Princess'* before she had her accident, withdrew from public life and the narrative had changed. The criticisms starting.

What if, at those times, they'd had someone like Lena to show the world who they really were?

'You're not unimportant, Lena.'

She looked up at him, a gentle smile teasing her lips. Barely there, but the hint was enough. The look of pleasure at his comment. It flooded him with sensation, something warm and bright, of wanting to make her smile more often. When had he ever felt like this, enjoying the simple pleasure of making a person happy?

Never, and he craved more of it.

He looked down on her, hair long and loose about her shoulders. Her skin smooth and golden. Plush lips a soft pink. So fresh and beautiful. The collar of his normally comfortable shirt became too tight, the room too hot. Even though he knew his rooms were perfectly climate controlled, he wanted to throw open a window and let in the cool night air. Instead, he took another sip of his drink. The heat of the whisky burned, hitting his stomach.

'And you're not unimportant either—what you think, what you feel,' Lena said. 'So where does the ambassador get off raising marriage with the man who's one day going to be his king?'

There was a sharpness to her voice, a story there that he wanted to hear. And he found he wanted to know a great deal more about her. Her likes, dislikes. Her passions...

'I assume it's a message from my parents—a not so subtle hint via their friend, if you will.'

'Our parents and their desire for children to marry to solve all their problems.'

'You've had experience of this?' he asked.

The corner of her mouth kicked up. It wasn't a smile. There was sadness in that wry kind of grin of hers.

'My mother thought if I married it'd sort out her issues.

It didn't seem to matter what I wanted, so I'm familiar with the sensation.'

'What did your father think?'

Something about her closed off immediately. One minute her face was open. Warm. Sympathetic. The next, it was as if she were made of glass. Cool and brittle.

'My father's dead.'

He started forward, an ache in his chest. Feeling terrible for bringing back painful memories.

'I'm so sorry.'

She shrugged. 'He wasn't much of a father. More a donor of genetic material. I'm surprised you don't know that already, what with the investigations your palace would have done to ensure I…fit.'

He guessed she was right and that she'd been investigated closely, but he hadn't bothered looking into it. If Lena had been cleared to come to an interview with him, the relevant checks hadn't shown up anything of concern.

'You'd have been vetted when you went to work with Isolobello's royal family. Priscilla recommended you. That was enough for me. But I want to know what problems your mother thinks your marriage might solve.'

If there was something he could help with, it might ease the pressure on Lena. He didn't know why he hated that thought—of her marrying someone else, whereas at the same time, he had an intense desire to see her in a wedding dress, a veil over her face, looking up at him… No, not at him. That was *not* where his thoughts were going. She was a beautiful woman, that was all, and she'd make a beautiful bride.

The air in the room seemed to get still and heated again.

He shrugged off his jacket and draped it over the arm of the chair, loosened his tie and undid the top button of his shirt. Lena took another sip of her hot chocolate, then licked her lips, the pupils of her eyes wide and dark in the lower light of the room. Something heavy, palpable, weighed on him—the intensity of the situation, the desire to kiss her, to taste her. It was wrong. He was her employer. Yet, he also accepted in that moment that he was simply a man, and she was a beautiful woman. And what man wouldn't want to kiss her, wouldn't want to marry her, wouldn't want to have her for ever?

But she remained quiet, the question unanswered.

'That employment trial, your probation,' he said.

Her eyes widened, her white teeth biting into her lower lip.

'I think we both know you've passed it. I'll ask my private secretary to have the official employment contracts drawn up.'

Her mouth broke into the most beautiful smile. Whilst he'd seen her smile before, this one was pure, unrestrained joy. It lit her whole face.

'Thank you,' she said, her eyes glittering. Were those tears? 'You can't know what this means to me.'

She came closer to him, a step. Did he step towards her as well? Gabe wasn't sure. He might have imagined it, but he could almost feel the warmth from her body. His own, too hot. Everything tight, as if he were too big for his skin, as if he wanted to split in two and morph into something, somebody else. They were almost touching now, so close if he leaned down he could capture her mouth with his own. He might have imagined it, but her head tilted back. Lips sightly parted. He wanted to kiss her. Craving it more than his next breath. Did she want to kiss him?

A gentle rap sounded at the door, and the handle turned. The door cracked open, and Lena stood back. There was only one person who would ever walk in, the only other individual who had any entitlement to be in his personal quarters and space. One he'd texted after he'd arrived back at the house—his valet.

'Pieter,' he said.

'Y-Your Highness.' Gabe didn't miss the slight hesitation. 'I can leave—'

'No,' Lena said. 'We were talking work, and it's late, but maybe...' She placed her cup on a side table and reached into the back pocket of her jeans, pulling out her phone. 'We can take photographs of some unscripted moments. The public like you unscripted.'

Unscripted. He wanted to know—was that what she liked about him too? But these thoughts led nowhere.

'So what would you like us to do?' Pieter said, completely unfazed.

'What would you normally do at this time?' Lena asked.

'Get undressed,' Gabriel said.

'Oh.' She gave a low and soft kind of chuckle, a sexy kind of sound that shot through his blood more potently than any of the whisky he'd drunk tonight. 'Well, those kinds of photos would cause even more of a stir in the comments section than we have so far.'

Pieter chuckled too. 'I should read some of them to you, sir. They are quite the thing.'

Lena cocked her head to the side, studying him. Did she pick up on what Pieter had said? Who knew. Yet he wanted her to admire him, to like him. Little else seemed as important.

'What caused this?' he asked, totally bemused.

'The photograph of you and Carl. Nothing more enticing, it seems, than a man and child. But don't worry, whilst a shirtless shot would give the Internet a coronary and launch your popularity into the stratosphere, we are *not* giving them that.'

There was a sound to her voice. Something a little sharp. Almost protective. Could it be...possessiveness? He liked that it might be.

'Just...pretend I'm not here for a bit,' Lena said. Didn't she realise how impossible that concept was? There was no way he could ignore her. Every time she was in his presence he experienced an intoxicating prickle of awareness. Something that drew his attention to her, like a compass to magnetic north.

He tried to do what she asked. Pieter seemed to have no trouble ignoring her, but that was his training. His employer was his focus, no one else. Gabe didn't know why he wanted the same focus from Lena, yet perhaps that was what he had, though always through a lens. Her eyes trying to find the essence of him.

What if she stopped seeing him through that lens and started seeing him for real?

'Did you have a good evening, Your Highness?' Pieter asked as they walked towards the dressing room where his clothes hung.

'You know how the ambassador is.'

'Of course.'

Pieter didn't need to say anything more. He'd been with

Gabriel long enough to know exactly what Gabe thought of the ambassador here. Gabriel pulled off his tie, handed it over to his valet. Gabe was quite capable of looking after himself yet, somehow, talking to Pieter was like a debrief. Though he felt as if he didn't need it tonight, that he'd already debriefed with Lena…

Pieter took the tie and hung it on a tie rack.

'I'll get His Highness wearing a pink tie one day,' Lena said, the amused, lilting sound of her voice like fingers traced gently down his spine.

'I'd like to see you try, Ms Rosetti.' Pieter sniffed, although Gabe knew him well enough to glean the amusement in his voice too. Saw the merest of smiles on his usually impassive face. Gabe didn't know why he wanted his longest-serving employee to like his newest, yet he didn't dwell. A harmonious workplace was good for everyone, that was all.

In a strange way, Gabe felt adrift. Separate. As if he weren't a part of what was going on here. It was an uncomfortable sensation. He didn't know how long it had been since he'd truly felt part of something. Sure, he was a member of the royal family. He was close to his siblings, but Ana and Cilla had moved on with their lives. Some might have seen them as a close family but he'd never had an easy, warm relationship with his parents. Most of the time they'd dictated to their children, and Gabe and his sisters simply followed. Even his moniker, the Proper Prince, spoke volumes about him. It told of a person who always stood apart.

The only time he'd felt a real sense of belonging, he realised, was when he'd played football. The ease of it. He hadn't been a prince then, he'd been a team member. All with a common purpose, sure, but a camaraderie as well. He removed the cufflinks from one sleeve, then the other. Placed them on a dressing table. Looked over at Lena, glowing in the soft, warm light of the lamps. Holding her phone. Doing what? Taking stills? Video? It was such a strange sensation to be having his life catalogued like this. What did she see, or think, when she looked at him? Did she want him to undress in front of her? Something about having Pieter here seemed so clinical and cold, when all Gabe craved was heat. He'd felt that heat with her, before Pieter had arrived. Why couldn't he have it again?

Because she was his employee, and Gabe knew that their situation was impossible.

His shirt felt too rough against his skin. He wanted to be naked, exposed to the cool night air. Not trapped in this suit that had begun to feel foreign to him. He undid the second button of his shirt. A third. Lena stilled. Something crackled in the air, a kind of electricity. It wasn't Lena in the room forgotten right now, but his valet.

She seemed to hesitate. Stopped what she was doing, looked at the screen of her phone.

'I think I have enough. Is there anything you'd like me to say on a post about your night tonight?'

'I'm sure you'll think of something that doesn't involve my telling the ambassador to keep his opinions to himself.'

Lena nodded. Gave a brief curtsey. 'Noted. Goodnight, Your Highness. I—I'll see you tomorrow, for your meeting at the palace.'

She turned and it was almost as if she fled the room, leaving her cup of hot chocolate behind. The faintest, tantalising pink smudge from her lips on the rim.

CHAPTER FIVE

LENA HAD CHECKED her compact mirror earlier, noting that all attempts to hide the dark circles under her eyes had failed. She wondered how they were shaping up now, after two hours at their morning engagement. Last night she'd barely had any sleep after her moment with Gabriel. She didn't understand it, the electric attraction that had seemed to sizzle between them. It was as if the feeling was something necessary to her very being. She craved it again. That need to simply be close to someone when she'd never really wanted it before. She couldn't shut down her mind, the memories of the feel of his embrace on the terrace, even though it had happened by accident. That moment in his room where they were so close she could almost feel his breath on her face. The way he looked down at her, eyes full of heat.

No, she couldn't think about it, yet that didn't stop the truth that she wanted him. An unsettling feeling when she'd never really wanted anyone before, not like this at least. She'd never really trusted enough, but there was something she trusted about him… It was almost as if he *saw* her, more than just as his employee, but as a person he might trust too. Lena took a deep breath to settle her racing heart. She had to keep focussed on her job.

The picture from last night had been received well. How couldn't it have been? With him, backlit in the low light of his room. Tie off, top button undone. Removing the cufflinks from his shirt. Such an intimate moment, which she hadn't thought about when she'd posted it in a fluster. She almost couldn't bear to read the comments so had asked Gabe's private secretary to scan them to see if there was anything that needed to be deleted. She was almost at the stage of needing a junior employee to help manage the account, so many people were beginning to follow. He'd said there was nothing, but was amused at the hashtag trending in the comments, *hashtag thirst-trap* as it related to their boss.

Thirst trap indeed.

She was parched dry just being around him, trying to do her job.

Now they were heading to the car to another meeting. Gabriel's shoes crunching on the gravel drive under his purposeful stride. His private secretary was planning to travel ahead to prepare. Lena almost wanted to join Henri, yet she didn't have an excuse to change the arrangements. She'd be left alone in the vehicle with Gabriel instead, with that scent of his, all fresh and evergreen. She almost couldn't breathe at the thought.

'Sir, I've loaded the documents into your reader for the next engagement. Is there anything else you need?' Gabriel's private secretary asked.

The crunch of Gabriel's shoes on the drive faltered, then quickly picked up to the same rhythm again. Reader? What was that about…?

'No, Henri. There's nothing else. I'll see you there. Lena, what are your plans for the next talks?'

Gabriel was all business this morning, not a shred of softness in him. No doubt regretting the moment between them last night. He was looking sharp in a navy suit, white shirt, and a yellow and blue tie echoing the colours of Halrovia's flag.

'I thought I'd take a photograph of you and the defence minister shaking hands in front of the countries' respective flags.'

They were attending bilateral security talks. Not that Halrovia or Lauritania had been in conflict with anyone for almost a century, but she guessed it was a show of solidarity and closeness of ties.

'Excellent,' Gabriel said, glancing down at her feet, which were in low-heeled shoes today after yesterday's debacle. Was he remembering her clumsiness on the terrace? How he'd worn a cup of coffee, and, for a little while, her? She couldn't tell, his expression hidden behind his sunglasses. Lena's cheeks flared with heat.

Before she could respond, her phone rang. She checked the number. Her mother? Lena's stomach twisted in complicated knots. They'd had some text exchanges when she'd taken this job. She'd kept in touch with her brother to make sure that he was still in university and studying. That there was food on the table and the bills were being paid, because her mother was useless at that sort of thing, never having had to worry about money in the past. Lena was tempted to decline the call, but she needed to know what was happening and her mother was terrible at texting. It would be easier to get it over with by speaking to her.

'Sir, I need to take this call,' she said as she swiped to

answer. 'I'll meet you at the car in a few moments. We're ahead of schedule so you won't be late.'

He nodded, and strode on as Lena stopped in the shade.

'Mama…' Lena said. She couldn't get any other words out before her mother started.

'The landlord is increasing the rent.' Her mother's voice was tremulous, panicked. Lena's heart sank. This was bad news. She'd told her mother that she should leave her home because they couldn't afford it, but her mother had been so upset with the death of Lena's father and all that had happened, Lena had agreed to give her time. She'd given her mother and brother the money she would have spent on her own rent to cover some of the cost, topping it up with her wages. It left her with very little for herself, but she had accommodation and didn't have many needs. She could be frugal…except now, this would leave everything short.

Lena's chest tightened. She took a deep breath, wondering when it would ever end. Would she be responsible for her mother for ever? It seemed wrong. Her mother was an adult and wasn't her responsibility. Though there was her brother too… The burn of acid started in her belly as her thoughts whirred.

'When?'

'In eight weeks. What do I…?'

'You have to leave. There's *no* other choice. I'm at work now but I'll sort something out.'

'You don't get paid enough in this role. You could always—'

'No, I couldn't.'

She knew what her mother was about to say. *Marry.* Her mother claimed there were any number of men who would be interested on certain specialised dating sites for just that kind of thing. Rich men who'd look after her. Her family. The bile rose to her throat. She swallowed it down.

'I—I have had some other job offers. Maybe one will pay me more. We'll talk later, I promise. But everything will be okay.'

'You say that, and it hasn't been since your father died.' Her mother's voice cracked as she hung up.

Tears pricked at Lena's eyes. She wiped them away. She didn't believe Queen Lise had been joking about the job, should she want one, and she bet that King Rafe would offer her a premium to leave Gabriel. Yet that wasn't what she wanted. She'd committed to this job, *loved* this job. Felt as though she finally had a place.

There was more to do, that was all, and Lena never wanted to leave work half done. She was only now starting to get traction. Really achieving something. Turning the tide of press opinion as Gabriel's PR and image advisor, rather than as a junior part of a team, as she'd been on Isolobello. If she succeeded, it would make her career. A glowing reference from two royal families would mean she could go anywhere in the world for work, ask her own price. It was what she'd always wanted. Independence, security.

Wasn't it?

No decisions needed to be made right now. She could think about it a little later. Gabriel *needed* her, just as Cilla had said. Today, she had a job to do and would do it the best way she could, with dedication and focus. Lena checked her mascara and wiped away a few smudges, then began walking to the official vehicle. As she rounded the corner of the building what she saw in front of her brought her to a halt.

On an expanse of grass were a group of men kicking a

football in the sunshine. Workers, she guessed, on a lunch break. They laughed as the ball was passed around, though that wasn't what caused her to stop. It was Gabriel, at the edge of the grass. Standing, watching.

To others, his expression might have seemed impassive, but she knew him better now. The corners of his lips barely turned up. The intent way he stared at the men, as if getting ready to spring into action. She stood back, watching the tableau in front of her. She'd seen him, of course, in her research. The young man leading his country to a junior world championship win. The photos then, showed a person not yet grown into himself. Still tall, yet somehow rangier. Less bulk on him.

He'd grown into himself now, in every way.

The men on the grass were clearly in competition of some sort, friendly as it was. One team manoeuvred the ball around, trying to score a goal, whilst others shouted at each other in a friendly kind of banter. They were all young, fit. Some were muscular. But Gabriel was the one who held her attention. She couldn't take her eyes from him. Yet there was something about *how* he watched. It almost looked nostalgic, the way he was so solid whilst the action swirled in front of him. In that moment she didn't think. She raised her phone, set her camera app to video, and pressed record.

One of the men aimed for the goal close to Gabriel. Missed. The ball speared towards him. His leg shot out and he stopped the ball dead with one foot, in a way that even her untrained eye could tell was with an uncommon kind of skill.

The men on the grass looked at him, and everything paused, as if the world held its breath. Then almost as if out of muscle memory, he started forwards, kicking the ball in front of him. Lena was transfixed by the brilliance of it, as he cut through the men trying to intercept him, to take the ball away. It was as if they were nothing more than mere ir-ritations as he weaved between them, heading for the goal at the opposite end of the grass. Time slowed as she watched him dodge his assailants' attempts to tackle him. Then, in a moment almost even beyond her explanation, faced with a wall of men all joined together against him, their own teams forgotten, he lined up the ball and kicked. It flew, curved through the air in a sharp arc and hit the back of the goal net as Gabriel watched.

The men around him exploded in whoops and cheers, running towards him. Here, on this patch of grass, they were all equal. Lena forgot what she was doing, caught up in the sheer thrill of the scene in front of her. Then after a few moments it was as if he came back into himself. Gabriel turned. If she'd been asked, she would have said his expression was one of pure elation. A smile like she'd never seen before, splitting his face. Warm, true, joyous.

One that speared right into the heart of her, and in that moment, she *saw* him. Not His Royal Highness, Prince Gabriel, but Gabe Montroy, the man. It hit her as sure and true as if he'd kicked that football right into her solar plexus.

Something about him had changed. He seemed...*more*. As if he'd grown out of himself, shed an unwanted skin and somehow come alive. So unlike the man she'd met at her job interview. It was as if he'd become another person entirely. Sure, there was an ego about him. He'd be ruler of his country one day and would always carry that naturally superior demeanour with him, but this was something else.

Heat crept over her, that awareness again. Not of him as her employer or a future king, but of him as a man. Everything about him seemed larger than life. The way he fitted his clothes. His shoulders, broad and strong under his suit jacket. He seemed to become like some mythical figure. A god. His hair gleaming golden in the sunshine. All of him burnished. Beautiful. She stopped recording as he was feted by the other men. She didn't know if Gabriel could speak their language, but it didn't matter. Something about this moment seemed universal.

She took pleasure in simply watching as the men gave him the ball again and again in different positions on the expanse of grass, watching him kick goal after goal. Always the same perfect arc. Hitting the back of the net every time. She took a few still shots and some of the men had pulled out their phones too. Did they know who they played with? They had to be aware he was someone important. It was written all over him in the fit of his clothes, the way he held himself. You couldn't mistake him for anything other than a leader, yet in this moment there was a camaraderie. Prince or pauper, it didn't matter.

The game, such as it was, seemed to have wound up. Gabe shook hands with the workers, and they slapped him on the back. Made noises of disappointment about him having to go. She hadn't wanted to disturb anyone because they had plenty of time, but she still walked over to him, attracted like iron filings to a magnet. Watching as the workmen resumed their day and Gabe stood, distant and apart from it once more.

There was something about the moment that seemed poignant. Her heart beat an unsteady, excited kind of rhythm at what she'd witnessed. At the sheer *mastery* of him. He loomed so large right now, it was as if she were dwarfed. Then Gabriel focussed on her, and Lena noticed his breathing was a bit heavy, his shirt clung a little with perspiration from a workout in the bright sunshine.

'Y-you're *really* good,' she blurted out, the words spilling from her lips as the heat rose in her cheeks.

The corners of his mouth curled into a lazy smile, blinding and bright. Brimming with a magnificent kind of confidence in his own ability. He slid off his sunglasses and pinned her with his blue gaze that seemed to burn hot like a pilot light.

'I know,' he said. Winked.

And Lena went up in flames.

Gabe had always had a sense of place in the world, an awareness that he'd one day be King. Yet he'd somehow forgotten himself. Forgotten the boy he'd once been, filled with excitement at life and what lay ahead. The camaraderie of his team, whereas of late he'd felt so alone. The joy of a perfect kick, watching the ball curve and hit the back of the net. Of *winning*.

Of course, he'd won at life. He was a prince. He had all the privileges that his position entailed. Still, every day, someone wanted to carve a piece from him. The criticism, the barbs. Sometimes veiled, often not. Whilst he'd always carried a healthy sense of ego about what he could achieve for his people, he was only human. This moment just passed was simple, pure, and if he had to describe it, exhilarating. He didn't have to think, he simply *was*. It was as if he'd never walked away from the field. The memory of it came back to him. Made his blood pump hard and hot. He felt too big for his own skin. Alive again, as he hadn't been in years.

Especially with the way Lena was looking at him. He'd felt her gaze, as palpable as a caress. Now? Her cheeks carried a subtle blush, her eyes glittering. Pupils big and dark in the fathomless blue of her irises. Hair long and flowing round her shoulders like a river of dark silk that he craved to bury his fingers in to see if it was as soft as it looked.

He'd known she was watching him, and he'd wanted to perform for her. Driven to show her who he'd once been. Or perhaps, who he truly was when you stripped Prince Gabriel to his essence, and all that was left was the man.

'I—I had no idea.' That slight flush washed over her cheeks again.

The way she looked at him. He wanted to take her in his arms again, yet this time, to kiss her. Stake a claim, because he'd seen the way the workmen had looked at her. The admiration, the desire. Lena Rosetti was an exquisite woman and a man would have to be dead inside not to notice. He wasn't dead, not any more. He'd never felt more alive. As if he were King of the whole world.

'It's not hidden. I thought your research on me would have turned it up.'

'It did. It's just seeing it for real. That was…*something*. Why did you stop if you were that good?'

Because he'd been young and foolish and had felt untouchable. He'd become involved with someone he should never have trusted, and in the end that was the deal his parents had made with him. They'd dealt with the threats they never wanted to see the light of day. That he might be a hero on the football field, but he had trouble reading. In exchange, he went to work in the royal family. Who would challenge the story of a young man turning his back on everything he loved to serve his people?

If he thought hard about it and how his parents had behaved since, it was as if they didn't trust him. Neither did some of the press, not any more, though for spurious reasons. The bitter truth was that for so long he hadn't trusted himself. Questioned his own abilities because too much in his family had been unspoken. There were the frowns and thin-lipped disappointment of his parents when his school results had come in, yet they'd never asked why, only told him to try harder, as if he'd been lazy. In those times he'd wondered how he would ever be able to run a country when he had trouble making out words on a page. If he was seen as a failure…

The cut of his nails into his palms brought Gabe back from those thoughts into the present. He unclenched fists he didn't remember tightening. No. He *knew* he was trustworthy and didn't really care what other people thought of him, but deep in his soul he craved for someone who mattered to believe it. To trust him, and for him to trust them.

'I had a duty. I did what was expected of me. The burdens of my station.' Or so his parents said. Yet why did their children always have to be the ones that carried that burden for the crown?

'Was it what you wanted?'

Gabe checked the time. They needed to move to the next meeting, yet he didn't want to go. Not feeling like this. He wanted to relish the moment for a while, yet he still started walking because what was left for him but the duty to his country, which now felt like chains? He'd never been freer than on the field. It was what his sports master at school had realised after Gabe had struggled with reading and numbers and had been angry with the world because no one had worked out earlier why that was.

Then, when they had, hiding it from everyone as if it were an irrelevance when it was *everything* to him. He was tired of the dread he'd felt on entering a library. Of not being able to share the simple pleasure of sitting down and reading a book he held in his hands without feeling as though he was somehow lacking.

'What I wanted didn't matter.'

There'd not been a second's thought from his family. The utter dismissal still rankled, late at night when he lay awake, thinking of Halrovia's future and how he might shape it for the good of his people.

'It *does* matter.'

His feet crunched on the gravel beneath them, his footfalls faster and faster as if to escape the feelings swirling round him. Yet all he heard in Lena's sentence was, *You matter.* He didn't know why it hit him like a blade through the heart. An aching, needy thing that had no place in his life, and yet, he still held on to it tight, no matter the stabbing pain it unleashed.

'It's going to be years before you're King. Would it have mattered so much if you'd had an international football career?'

It had to his parents. So much about him mattered to them, but never his wants or needs. His dyslexia, his desire to play football professionally, to see what he could achieve. All meaningless. *'It's common!'* his mother had said about his request to at least try out for an international football career before his world had completely imploded with threats of betrayal.

'My parents and their private secretary felt a career in football was beneath my role as heir, and how it would be seen by Halrovia.'

A crease bisected Lena's brow as they walked past a formal garden. Clipped, restrained. Why did it remind him of himself, when all he wanted right now was colour and chaos?

Why did he want to shout out the real reason that he had to give up everything? The guilt he carried for it?

'With respect, sir, your parents' private secretary has done such a sensational job to date, I'm of the view he doesn't have a single clue about how you'd be seen by Halrovia. I mean, look at how well it's gone so far.'

The sarcasm poured hot and thick from her, though somewhat discordant with her attempt at formality. He couldn't help himself. He laughed. Around Lena, he seemed to want to laugh much of the time. What would his parents' private secretary think of this slip of a woman who had no tertiary education making that comment? Gabriel desperately wanted to see it, and see her cut him down to size. He'd bet the Halrovian kingdom that Lena would rival his mother in that skill if she really put her mind to it.

'I shouldn't have said that,' she whispered. 'I'm sorry.'

He suspected that she'd meant more than just his parents' private secretary too, that the criticism of his parents was implied as well.

Gabriel didn't much care.

'There's no need to apologise. I applaud honesty, and

you're right,' he said. 'Your employment is incontrovertible evidence.'

She cocked her head, pierced him with her vivid gaze. 'Do you trust me?'

'Yes.' He didn't have to think about that answer and a sense of relief swept over him. Whilst most people around him deferred to him because of duty, she didn't. He liked the challenge of her. The way she tried to find who he was, not accept what she'd been told or shown. And, in many ways, he knew that she had his back.

'That, there?' She waved her hand behind her. 'That's who people want to see...sir.'

Something seemed to have shifted. A kind of knowing. This formality between them, it felt *wrong*.

'Gabriel. In private, call me Gabriel.'

Her eyes widened. 'Okay...'

'So long as you're comfortable with the invitation.' In her role she'd likely be witness to some of his most intimate and vulnerable private moments, and it felt wrong to maintain this false formality between them.

'I am... Gabriel.'

It was like being thrown in a blast furnace. The sound of his name slipping from her lips as she tried it out. Did she like saying it? He couldn't understand why he wanted to know so badly. He shrugged the strange sensation off. It was nothing. He'd offered the same to his private secretary, who'd politely refused because he didn't feel it was right. However, Lena wasn't from Halrovia. He wasn't going to be her king, so it mattered less.

Or that was what he was trying to convince himself...

'Excellent.'

He wasn't a man who dwelled too much on his decisions, but he was likely to ruminate over this one and, for that, he needed time.

'So,' she said as they approached the car. 'I took a video.'

'Really.' He didn't know what he thought about that, only that he quite liked that she seemed to have enjoyed what she'd seen enough to video it.

'As I said, it was…impressive.' Her vivid blue eyes seemed to darken. 'And given you said you trust me… I'd like to post it to your social media pages.'

His heart missed a beat. For a few seconds he had to think about how that made him feel. His football had been a loss. He'd tried to set it aside, even though in the end he still did some practice because he'd loved the game. Showing that side of him again? In many ways it left him exposed, reminding him of a time that was raw and painful. One he didn't really want to talk about.

'Do you want to go viral?' Lena asked, perhaps sensing his hesitation for reasons even he couldn't fully articulate. Yet, why not? It was what Lena had been employed for. She wanted to, and he believed in her judgement. She hadn't been wrong yet.

'Let's do it.'

She smiled, and it was a glorious thing. Full of warmth and happiness. Her eyes dancing with excitement. Was it because she was doing her job and was happy to be doing it well? Or was it that he'd given her *proof* that he trusted her? Gabe wasn't sure, even though he enjoyed her smile. Took it as a precious gift bestowed upon him.

'You've been working hard, and the results speak for themselves. Even my parents' secretary seems happy.' As if that were any yardstick. 'I have the state dinner tonight so you can take the rest of the day off.'

'Thank you, si— Gabriel.'

Gabe rarely second-guessed his decisions. Even though they'd failed him in the past, he'd honed his instincts on sharp and brutal experience and, now, they were invariably right. Still, hearing Lena say his name did something to him. It was like the sultriest music. It started a drumbeat of desire deep and low.

Perhaps he enjoyed the sound of his name from her mouth just a little too much.

CHAPTER SIX

LENA STROLLED THROUGH the dimly lit halls of the lake home, as she'd begun calling it. Today, she'd taken advantage of the time off Gabriel had given her. Exploring Lauritania's antique markets in the old, walled part of town. Having a lovely dinner out with a couple people from work who had accompanied the royal tour; a personal protection officer who'd had the night off too, and Gabriel's private secretary. They'd drunk a glass of champagne each, toasting the success of the trip, which was now drawing to a close. Eaten at a quaint little restaurant with red and white checked tablecloths, tea-light candles on the table, and delicious rustic food. After dinner she'd left them partying and planning to hit the clubs, whilst she'd returned home.

All the while, she had a prickling sensation of something missing. As if she shouldn't be celebrating. Was it…guilt? She had so much to think about. Her mother's situation. How to manage it on her current wage. Should she contact Albert at the Lauritanian palace and ask if Queen Lise was serious about a job? Everything about her revolted at the idea, even though it would be best for her family. But what about her? Shouldn't she be able to do what she wanted, for once, without worrying about everyone else? She shouldn't feel this way. She *should* have been able to enjoy herself like any normal young woman. Gabriel had given her the night off.

Gabriel…

She *liked* saying his name. Liked that he'd invited her to use it when in private. As if it was some secret between them. Lena knew she shouldn't be reading too much into it but something about the moments between them recently had seemed special.

He was handsome, self-deprecating. Kind, and he cared. He trusted her and she found that, despite everything, she trusted him too. He'd be a wonderful king one day. And she began to wonder, had anyone ever told him that? *Gabriel, you'll make a great king.* Lena only wished that the world could see it as she did. She felt the weight of her role, wanting to present him at his absolute best, because the public deserved to know him as she saw him. She'd do everything in her power to show them all.

It was like a fire lit inside her, that sense of protectiveness. But there was something more. Desire. A heat and need whenever she was around him that threatened to overwhelm her and burn away all common sense.

Dangerous, Lena. Dangerous.

There could never be anything between him. He was her employer, a *prince*. There was no risk of love here. She'd never much trusted the emotion anyhow, because look at how well it had gone for her mother. Spending a lifetime sharing a man, for what? But perhaps this was what made Gabriel the safest person of all, because she couldn't expect anything from him. His position wouldn't allow it, and that would protect them both.

She walked past his wing on the way to the kitchens to

get a cup of hot chocolate before bed. Hesitated. Stopped. Turned around as if drawn. Her feet carrying her back along the path she'd just come, deeper into his section of the home. Wondering if he'd returned from the state dinner yet. How it had gone. Maybe he'd want to talk with someone about it?

As she approached his suite, Lena glimpsed a sliver of light under his door. She turned towards it, her feet seeming to carry her without much thought, just the sensation that she was being pulled in his direction. An itch under her skin telling her she needed to do this. Before he'd left tonight, he'd looked tired. So very tired.

She supposed trying to shore up your allies and improve your unfairly falling reputation carried significant pressures, not to mention your own ambassador suggesting you marry when it was none of his damned business. She understood being buried under the weight of obligation after her father had died. When she'd realised her whole life would have to change. The fight to find another job, the recognition that she was responsible for her family and their future. Putting aside her own dreams. What would it be like, instead, to be responsible for a *country*?

Maybe Gabriel would have preferred to come out to a simple dinner too. Sharing a glass of champagne and laughter in a little corner restaurant with no care.

Lena knocked. Waited. Listened, barely able to hear anything over the thudding heartbeat in her chest. Then one word.

'Yes.'

She cracked open the door and continued down a short entrance hall towards the lounge area of his suite, following the dim light. She almost didn't see him, standing still at the far end of the room. In a formal shirt, the top few buttons undone. Bow tie draped carelessly around his neck. His arm propped on the mantelpiece, almost negligently holding a tumbler of amber fluid. Head dropped. It looked as if the mantelpiece was the only thing holding him up. As if his glass was about to slip from his fingers.

A wiggling sensation started in her belly, like a flock of a thousand birds taking wing. One look at him took her breath away, because he was one of the most beautiful men she'd ever seen. Although tonight, he seemed...vulnerable. Standing there as if undone. She wanted to go to him, offer comfort, offer him everything.

Though, no matter how he looked right now, what she'd come to learn over her time working with him was that his restrained exterior wasn't evidence of coldness. It was just he'd never been allowed to be himself, because his parents and courtiers wanted the best parts of him suppressed. The parts of him that people would relate to. His personality. His feelings.

Gabriel was no automaton. He was a man with passions who should have been allowed to show them.

'I... It's late.' Lena didn't know why she said it. She should have turned and walked away, leaving him to his own thoughts, but something about tonight told her that he needed some company as much as she did.

His head shot up, flinty blue gaze fixed on her. Even in the dim light of the room she could *feel* it prickling into her.

'*Lena.*'

The way he said her name. The rasp of it. The rough sound scraping like fingernails over her skin. If she hadn't known better, she might have thought his voice was filled with need. Maybe she needed him too.

This thing between them, it seemed to have taken on a life of its own. Bigger than both of them. The way he looked at her right now, so stark, so intense and burning as if he'd branded her, let Lena know that she hadn't imagined it.

'Gabriel.'

He took a swig from his drink. Placed the empty glass on the mantelpiece. Looked her up and down, in a way that could have been admiring. She wasn't sure. Tonight, she'd dressed to go out. Another wrap round dress. This one of soft, printed silk in jewelled colours, with beaded accents around the neck. Ruffles round the hem. It drifted about her as she walked and made her feel feminine. Pretty. Sure, the neck plunged a little lower than she normally wore but she'd never heard anyone complain before.

'You've been out.' The words sounded almost accusatory.

'It's what you do when you're given the night off by your employer.'

He almost flinched at the word, as if he didn't want reminding of who he was.

'Did you have fun?'

'Yes. Henri, Serge and I went to a little café in the old town. They wanted to continue the party. I came back here.'

'I'm glad…' She stiffened and the moment held, pregnant with possibility. 'Glad that you had a good time.'

Of course he'd want her to have a good time. It wasn't that he was glad she was back here with him. Was it?

'What are you doing here?' he asked.

'I—I saw the light. I came to see how tonight went.'

His shoulders slumped. He shrugged. 'It was a typical state dinner.'

'Well, I've never been to one of those so I can only guess. Were you seated next to anyone interesting?'

'Being the guest of honour, I sat with the King and Queen. It was a sumptuous feast with beautiful food and wine showcasing Lauritania's finest producers. The Grand State Dinner service was used. I'm told there were over a hundred candles lit for the meal.'

The whole evening sounded incredible, but he recounted what went on as if he were reading a funeral notice.

'No eligible princesses?'

That stark look returned. 'There are always eligible princesses, or daughters of dukes, marquesses, earls, counts, viscounts, barons. You name it, they're there.'

'Sounds like a fruit salad of peerage.'

'I'll never think of them the same, ever again.' Gabriel chuckled, but it wasn't a happy kind of sound. 'A veritable cornucopia, although many of them aren't as colourful or sweet as fruit.'

There was that tired sound to him again. She stepped forwards, closer. Wanting to reach out, put her hand on his arm. To touch, to comfort. To…more. Say everything was going to be okay, even though she didn't know what was wrong.

'You don't sound like you enjoyed yourself.'

'Lise and Rafe are always engaging company, but… I wish you'd been there.'

As he said it, his gaze fixed on her but this wasn't something cool and impassive. It was full of heat. That look scorched her, igniting in her core and burning outward. She shouldn't be here. This was a mistake in every way, both on his part and on hers, and yet she couldn't move.

She'd spent enough time thinking of others, worrying about what they thought of her. It all felt like a millstone round her neck because she had begun to realise what she might have been holding onto wasn't a sense of responsibility, but of fear. Fear of being criticised, fear of being seen as somehow lacking. Lena was tired of it. Holding back. Being less. Her virginity, which was another thing she realised she'd clung to in an effort to protect herself. To allow someone into your body you had to trust them, and she realised she didn't really trust much at all.

Why would she? Her parents hadn't set great examples. Her mother choosing secrecy over the welfare of her own children and her father showing how fickle he was prepared to be. For so long she'd believed if that was how people treated each other in relationships and families then she wanted no part of it. Especially when everything in her life seemed to be secrets and lies.

Except for now. There was a kind of truth in this room. This…thing that seemed to be growing larger and more palpable. She'd begun to feel as if Gabe valued her, trusted her. And in the tumult of her emotions a tiny seed of something fragile had begun to sprout and grow inside her.

She might just trust him too.

'You look beautiful,' Gabriel said, then raked his hand through his no longer neat hair, displacing it until a curl flopped over his forehead. Rubbed his hands over his face. 'That was wrong of me. I shouldn't have said it. You need to go.'

She should. Lena knew it was the sensible thing to do,

but nothing would make her move backwards out of this room. She'd spent a lifetime trying to be good, be sensible, so that people would like her. Her father, her teachers, her schoolmates. And for what? That green shoot deep inside her grew leaf, blossomed. She felt so full, and so aching and empty at the same time. Instead of leaving, she moved forwards into him.

'What if I don't want to?'

He made a sound as if the air had been punched out of him. 'You should.'

'But I like that you wish I'd been with you, by your side. I like that you think I'm beautiful.'

'I'm your employer, you're my employee.'

'Before all of that I'm a woman.'

'Yes, you are unmistakably a woman. But there's a power imbalance here, and that doesn't make it fair on you.'

She put her hands on her hips, stared him down. She was tired of being seen as powerless. Right now, she was full to the brim with her sense of how powerful she truly was. An unfamiliar, intoxicating sensation.

'An imbalance? Why do you think I don't have *all* the power here? With a bad series of posts or saying the wrong thing, I could destroy your reputation irrevocably. Who has the power now, Gabriel? It seems that it's all with me.'

He pushed away from the mantelpiece and stalked towards her. Stern, intent. Goosebumps peppered her skin. A shivery kind of sensation overtook her, as if she were coming down with something, running hot and cold all over.

'You'd destroy me, would you?'

Her cheeks flushed. She wanted to protect him, not destroy him. Lena bit into her lower lip. 'Well, no, but I could.'

'What if you already have?'

A pulse started deep and low at her core. The relentless ache intensified inside her.

'Gabriel,' she whispered.

'I like the way you say my name. Say it again.'

'Gabriel.'

He clenched and unclenched his hands. Then Gabriel flexed his fingers as if itching to touch her but trying to hold back.

'A-are you expecting Pieter?' She knew if anyone walked in on them, the night would be over even before it began, and she didn't want to stop whatever might happen between them.

'No, I've given him the night off.'

They stood close now, as they had the evening before, free to see where things took them. Did she want this? The answer, clear in her head, was *yes*. She might see Gabriel, but she believed that he saw her too. Had chosen her. Valued her in a way she'd never been before. As Lena Rosetti, the woman.

The way Gabriel looked at her now. As if he were starved. As if she were the only woman left on earth. So intent... If she was going to lose her virginity, then why not with someone like him? Someone handsome, someone who stole her breath. Who thought of others. She was sure he'd take care—not that she was really planning to tell him about her virginity, but he seemed like the type of man who'd look after any woman he was with.

That thought stung. She didn't like the idea of him with anybody else, but knew that was the reality of who they both were. Perhaps she needed to reinforce it.

'I understand what this is. How it has to be.'

'Do you?' Gabe chuckled, but didn't sound very entertained. 'Because I'm not sure myself.'

'I'm not asking for promises. I realise that this is behind closed doors. And I have no expectations.'

'You sell yourself so short. Stop. You're worth more than you know.'

Her whole life she'd been waiting to hear those words. Confirmation of what she'd hoped, then believed. That Gabriel acknowledged her value as a person, when most of the time she'd felt either dismissed, or invisible. Finally, someone had given voice to an unmet need she'd carried for years. To be seen for who she was, to be seen as worthy. It was overwhelming, like a burden lifting, even if the sensation lasted for only a night.

'You have no idea what that means to me.' The burn of tears pricked at her eyes, and she blinked them away.

'I fear I do,' he said, 'and that makes the world an unfair place.'

Lena tilted her head up, and her lips parted. She craved his touch, his kiss. To do something to channel this emotion that was banked up inside her, though she had no idea how to initiate things. What to do with all the feelings threatening to overwhelm her.

'Life's unfair. We just have to snatch what joy and pleasure we can when it's offered, and live the rest the best way possible.'

Gabriel shut his eyes for a moment, took a deep, slow breath, then opened them again. It was as if something had changed. His jaw clenched, nostrils flaring in a kind of determination.

'You know what's bound to happen if you don't leave? You know where this is heading?'

'Yes.'

'Tell me you want it as much as I do.'

'I want you more than my next breath,' she said.

'Thank God.'

She wanted to lose herself in him, and his body. But she knew that she might just find herself as well. Although there were rules, she was sure. Unspoken ones, which she needed to voice.

'Gabriel, I know it's just for tonight. I know what we are—'

He placed a finger gently on her lips where it burned like a brand. His other hand settled on her waist as Gabriel slipped his arm around her, and she craved for him to touch every part of her, to kiss her, to fill the terrible emptiness gnawing deep inside.

'There's no difference between us. We're two people who want. Tonight's all we have, so I plan to give you the world for one evening,' he murmured as he dropped his head to hers, and their lips touched—his mouth soft, coaxing. The tenderness of him in this moment, as if giving thanks, as if fusing her to him. He tightened his hold and deepened the kiss. She opened for him, their tongues touching. She didn't have time to be shy. Sensation overwhelmed her. She pressed against his body, into the hardness of him, relishing his arousal, knowing she'd done this to such a magnificent man. It gave some truth to her statement that she had all the power here, though she felt the scales tipping at his masterful touch.

He pulled away. She didn't want to let him go. His breath came in heavy gusts. Gabe took her hand.

'What you do to me,' he said, and placed it on his groin. He was so hard—the feel of him made her ache inside. She clutched him and stroked through the fabric. He moaned, the sound deep and carnal, making her catch fire. Tremble with need.

'Come to bed. Let me make love to you,' he said.

There was only ever one answer for her.

'Yes.'

He swept her into his arms. This wasn't like the moment on the terrace. This was something else, purposeful, almost romantic, if she didn't know this was all they could have. He strode into the bedroom and placed her down gently at the end of the bed, looking at her feet in their strappy gold sandals.

'Shame there are no heels.'

Lena wanted to say *next time*, but there were rules and she'd stick by them. 'You just want me to fall into you so you can catch me. I know your style.'

He laughed deep and low, the sound rumbling right through her. 'I wanted to feel them digging into my back as you screamed in pleasure underneath me.'

Lena almost dissolved on the spot in a puddle of need. What could she say in response? She had nothing in her repertoire. Luckily Gabriel knew exactly what to do. He undid the tiny buttons at the side of her waist, holding her dress in place.

'You're like the most precious gift for me to unwrap.'

The front of the dress fell open. Then he moved forward

and unclipped the snap between her cleavage that kept the bodice together, trailing his lips up her neck to her ear.

'Beautiful,' he murmured as goosebumps showered over her skin.

Lena shivered with the pleasure of it. She wanted him to unwrap her, to unravel her, to pull her apart at the seams. She could put herself back together in the morning, but right now, she was thankful for his control. He reached to the other side of the dress, where ties held it together inside. Slowly, he undid one bow, then the next, until the skirt came apart, and he stood back, staring at her, his mouth partly open, looking deliciously dishevelled.

'I need to be inside you,' he said.

'I need that too.'

She didn't have any fear, even though this was her first time. He reached out and slipped the dress from her shoulders and it fell to the floor around her feet.

'Undo my shirt,' he commanded in a way that was so princely, she almost smiled. Thrilled to do as he asked. She began unbuttoning the studs on the front of his dress shirt till it was open. She'd seen pictures of him when he was younger, with his shirt off, but it was nothing like seeing him for real. The defined muscles of his pectorals, the washboard abdomen, which spoke of hard work and dedication to exercise, as she knew he applied to all parts of his life. Would apply to her. She pushed the shirt from his shoulders, resting her hands on the powerful muscles there for a moment, feeling all that strength, wondering how it would be when she was underneath him.

Trembling with the anticipation of it.

'Now my trousers.'

She reached her shaking fingers and undid the hook at the waist. Slowly undoing the zip, notch by notch, as he stood there, his gaze glassy, his breathing heavy. Once she was done, she reached inside and cupped him, feeling how hot he was, how large. She knew they'd fit. Human bodies were made for each other. But the size of him. Didn't she owe Gabriel to tell him that she'd never done this before? She squeezed slightly, testing him out.

'Temptress,' he hissed through gritted teeth, and she couldn't help but smile. She'd never seen herself that way and loved that was how he viewed her. She rested her hand on his chest, the slight dusting of hair there that bisected his abdomen and disappeared beneath the band of his underwear.

'There's something I need to tell you.'

'Contraception? I have condoms. I'm careful. I have regular health checks.'

'No.' She shook her head, 'You need to know… I've never done this before. I'm a virgin.'

'I'm a virgin.'

Gabriel stopped. He couldn't have heard correctly. Could he? But there'd been no ambiguity. This was… He'd never made love to a virgin before. The only time he thought he might have to was on his wedding night. And even then, it wasn't the sort of thing he'd ever sought out. A woman's past was her own. He'd never judge, since he believed everyone was entitled to pleasure, but this?

The sensations overwhelmed him. The privilege of her wanting him to be her first. The responsibility. Then all the questions. Such as why? Lena was a beautiful woman.

Men would clamour for her, even though in this moment he might have wanted to tear each of those men apart with his bare hands.

He looked down at her and he could see in her eyes. The way they were a little wider. The way she raked her lower lip through her teeth. Her vulnerability.

'I don't know what to say.'

'You don't have to say anything. It's not important. I just thought you should know if you wondered why I…'

Seemed inexperienced? He hadn't even thought about it, being so caught up in the moment. He took a step back to give himself space when all he wanted to do was to drag her closer.

'We shouldn't… You've clearly been waiting… You should—'

'No, I've been waiting for you.'

The heat roared over him like a wildfire. If he'd been aroused before it was nothing to how he felt now. He was so hard he could almost snap in two.

Lena wrapped her arms round her waist, another sign of the insecurity and innocence he'd not noticed before. 'I… maybe not you *exactly*…'

He wanted to chuckle, because she had a unique way of cutting him down, but feared that she'd think he was laughing *at* her, rather than at himself.

'I think you'll be nice to me. Take care of me. Make it good.'

She'd set the bar so low for herself. *Nice?* Was that all she hoped for? Part of his heart tore. Bled. He shouldn't be doing this, especially since her admission. And yet here she was, with complete power over him. Holding him in her thrall.

'Come here. Let me hold you.' He held out his hand.

She placed her own in his and he reeled her into him. Gabriel sat on the side of the bed and cradled her in his lap. She nestled into his body. He was so damned hard, desperate for her. Yet was torn between desire and doing the right thing.

She trembled in his arms. From desire, nerves or a combination of both, he couldn't tell. He stroked his hand up and down her spine, goosebumps peppering her skin under his fingertips. Gabriel kept up his ministrations. Caressing, soothing, till she melted into him.

'Why did you wait?' he asked.

'It's not important.'

'*You're* important, Lena.'

She let out a long, slow breath. 'It's not like I haven't dated a little, but I really wanted to concentrate on getting a career. Then…you know…men seemed only interested in me because I looked a certain way…'

'Beautiful, Lena. You're beautiful.'

'But they didn't really want *me*. They wanted who they imagined me to be.'

His hold on her tightened. The anger in his gut, volcanic at those kinds of men who didn't value her. Made her feel this way. He cupped Lena's jaw and she looked up at him, so open and wanting. This woman who trusted him. Who *chose* him. It was humbling.

'You deserve more than one night. You deserve to do this with a man who loves you.'

'My virginity's become this thing that hangs over me, that I don't want any more. This is *my* choice. No one else's. Anyhow, love's overrated. It seems who I want is you.'

There was a story there, but he was done. She'd entrusted

herself, her body, to him for his care. He'd honour that trust, her desires. Honour her. Still, Gabriel did what he believed was the right thing, even though all he wanted to do was throw her onto the soft covers and make love to her all night.

He gave her a chance to walk away. 'Lena, are you sure?'

She nodded.

'I need the words.'

'Yes, Gabriel.'

The way she said his name, fluttering soft as a moth's wing at midnight. She wanted him. He wanted her. It was a story old as time. His hands began moving with more purpose. Not to soothe, but to inflame. One cupping her breast, the pad of his thumb teasing at her nipple through her bra till it tightened to a hard nub. She began to writhe underneath at his attention, in his lap. Grinding into him, sending darts of pleasure through his overheated body.

How much better would it be when he had her under him? Dark hair spilling over the pillow. Head thrown back in ecstasy. He was so close. Gabe had little doubt he'd be transported to heaven, but he needed to make sure she was ready. Mindless in her craving for him.

'Let's get into bed.'

He let her go. She stood and he threaded his fingers through hers, leading her to the side of the bed where the covers had already been turned down for him. She toed off her pretty gold sandals, then moved to take off her bra. Hesitated.

'Leave it on,' he said. 'I'm so desperate for you I need to slow down. Make it good for you.'

She slid between the sheets, pulled the duvet over herself, enveloped by the soft down as she watched him. Looking so innocent. Lying there, exactly as he'd imagined, with hair like black ink on the pillow.

Gabe kicked off his own shoes. Shed his trousers and tossed them onto a chair. Left his underwear on. Lena's gaze tracked him. Her eyes widened a little when his trousers came off and the corners of her mouth tilted in a subtle smile he liked to believe was one of appreciation. He stood for a few moments, admiring her right back. Her eyes gleaming in the soft lamplight. Lips the pink blush of peaches. All the while he hoped he was allowing her to take in her fill of him. To adjust to the idea of his size. Hoping that she wouldn't be afraid.

It was his responsibility to ensure that she wasn't.

Gabriel moved onto the bed beside her, reaching out. Stroking a stray strand of hair from her face. Tracing the shell of her ear with his fingertips. Her eyelids fluttered shut. Lips parting in pleasure. Then he drew her close again, into his arms. Her body soft and pliant against his own. Captured her lips with his as she moaned. Kissing long and slow and deep. Tongues caught in a hypnotic rhythm as Lena flexed against him, as if she was trying to get closer.

Gabe reached round and undid the back of her strapless bra with a practised flick. Tossed it aside. He rolled Lena onto her back and went up on one elbow, looking down at her beautiful body. Palming her left breast in his hand. Stroking then pinching her nipple, which pebbled under his touch as Lena writhed restlessly. Panting. He dropped his head and laved her diamond-hard flesh with his tongue. She began whispering his name. Over and over. Interspersed with little cries of pleasure.

'Let's get these off you,' he murmured against her burning flesh. As hot as his own. Trying to concentrate only on her when he was at his breaking point. Thank God for his foresight to keep his underwear on, because all he craved to do was to plunge into her warm, wet flesh and lose himself. Yet there was time enough for that. They had a long night ahead of lovemaking should she gift him the privilege of her body more than once. He sat up. Slipped his hands into the sides of Lena's panties and slid them down her legs and off.

In all his late-night fantasises he'd never imagined some-one as enticing as her. Sprawled on the bed. Eyes glassy with desire. Golden skin and gentle curves, laid out for him. He bent down over her. Kissed her stomach. Lower. Lower.

'You're so beautiful.' Her scent was heady. A perfume of honey and chocolate with overlying arousal. Gabe reached the apex of her thighs.

'Open for me.'

Her legs fell apart and he slipped his tongue against the sweet, salt of her. Taking his time, finding the centre of her pleasure. Learning what made her gasp and cry out. The perfect rhythm. Teasing her till she was mindless. A prisoner to sensation.

When she was on the verge, the very cusp, he stopped.

'I'm going to touch you some more. Slide my fingers inside you. Get you ready for me.'

'Please, please.' Her voice was a chant. She lay before him almost wrecked. Her limbs lax. Glistening between her legs, so wet it almost undid him. Gabe climbed back up her body. Whilst he could have spent hours between her thighs holding her on edge till she begged, he wanted to be able to watch her. To make sure he could see her face so that if there was any hint of pain he could slow down, take his time.

His body ached to be inside her, but she'd trusted him with her first time and he'd ensure that it would ruin her for any other man. There'd be no one else. Something pricked in his conscience then, but he allowed himself to drown in those darkly possessive thoughts. They were fantasies, that was all. They hurt no one. Only heightened the pleasure.

And wasn't that what tonight was all about?

He dropped his mouth to Lena's nipple again. 'Let's try one finger.'

He teased her flesh with his tongue as he teased her entrance with his hand. She lifted her hips to match his rhythm. He had no doubt she ached for him to be inside her, so he slid one finger knuckle deep. She was so soft, hot, wet. Lena let out a sob. Gabe lifted his head to check on her but she lay there, eyes shut. Head arched back. A look of pained ecstasy on her face as he slid his finger in and out.

'Let's try two,' he murmured, and she moaned as he slid in another finger to join the first. Setting a steady rhythm. Working her tight flesh as he watched her lose herself to his touch.

He trembled with need like some teenager, yet refused to break his focus on her. The way a flush rose on her chest, up her neck, to her cheeks. The way her breath came in little pants. The flutter of her body on his fingers telling him she was close. Giving her time to adjust till he tipped her over the edge.

'There's a spot inside,' he said. His voice rough and unrecognisable to his own ears. 'You are going to enjoy this. Just feel, Lena. Nothing else but my hands and lips. Let yourself go.'

He curled his fingers forwards, found where he promised he would. Her eyes flew open but he wasn't sure she saw anything, the way her gaze was far away. Lost in her pleasure. He'd bring her back to him soon but, for now, he wanted to give her this. Pure bliss and nothing else.

He dropped his mouth to Lena's breast again.

'*Feel* what I'm doing to you.'

Then he captured her nipple in his mouth. Began teasing her clitoris with his thumb, his fingers deep, stroking inside. She arched her back. Stiffened. Stilled. He didn't change rhythm as Lena let out a high-pitched wail and broke around him. Her body convulsing with wave after wave of pleasure.

He continued, slowing as she began to sob. When her body relaxed, went limp, he took her gently in his arms and cradled her as she wept on his chest. Relishing the satisfaction of her first orgasm at the hands of another.

Of ruining her for ever.

Pleasure flooded over her like she'd never experienced. Lena felt broken, remade as she sobbed into Gabe's chest. He murmured gentle words that made little sense to her overwrought brain, other than recognising the tone. Gentle. Encouraging. Praising. The soft sentiments echoed by his hands on her skin. Soothing her. She'd never experienced anything like this. Didn't know how to process it. It had eclipsed anything she had ever known. She'd been mindless with it. Consciousness compressed to nothing but sensation.

'Okay?' Gabe murmured. She wanted to laugh. Just okay? This moment had changed her at an almost cellular level. A complete reconfiguration of who she'd understood herself to be. Lena wiped at her eyes. How must she appear now? Make-up a mess. Wrecked.

'I can't explain…'

He gave her a gentle smile. 'You don't need to. I understand.'

She didn't think he could.

Gabe kissed her cheeks. Her eyelids. Kissing away the tears. After what she'd experienced she couldn't imagine wanting more, but the minute his lips touched hers a wave of volcanic desire flooded over her. That need again, deep inside. For Gabe to fill her. She reached between them. Grasped him through his underwear. Stroked her hand up and down.

'Can I feel you?'

'Yes,' he said with a hiss. Sharp and pained. She reached beyond the band of his briefs, to the hot, hard skin. Marvelling at the silkiness of it. She needed to look, pushing the duvet back. Pulling his underwear down to watch what she was doing to him. Her hand moving. The ruddiness of him. A silvery bead of fluid forming at the tip. She craved to give him the same pleasure that he wrought from her. Lena looked up at Gabe's face. His eyes closed. Mouth part open. Breathing hard as if he couldn't get enough air.

As if he knew she watched him, Gabe opened his eyes, the intensity of desire in his normally cool gaze burning through her. This was a man who could have had anyone, and yet right now she literally held him in the palm of her hand.

She'd never felt more powerful, beautiful, wanted, as she did in this moment.

'I'd die to be inside you.'

'You don't have to go that far,' she said. Sliding her hands from his body and lying back, arching like a cat in the sun.

'Are you ready?' he asked. Manoeuvring out of his underwear. Tossing the briefs to the floor.

'Yes. I'm *aching*.'

His grin in response was pure wickedness. 'I can fix that for you. Make that pain go away.'

He turned to the side and opened a bedside drawer. Found protection. Rolled it on as she watched, unable to take her eyes from him. Then he was over her, his powerful body pressing her into the bed. She flexed her pelvis, rubbing herself against him. Eyes rolling back as his hardness met her soft, overheated flesh. He reached down between them. Stroked between her legs. She'd thought she'd be too sensitive but with a few gentle touches she was panting and begging for release.

'I want you. I can't wait to feel you. You're so beautiful…'

He kept up the words of encouragement as he notched himself at her centre. Began easing in with shallow thrusts.

'Lift up to me,' he said. His voice was rough and raw. Hand slipping under her backside as she tilted her pelvis and he slid deep inside.

He stilled. So did she. There was no pain, only pressure. A fullness. Their gazes clashed. She'd give everything to know what he was thinking, then he began to move and feeling took over.

'Do what's natural,' he said. 'Move. Lie there. Change position. Whatever gives you the most pleasure.'

Pleasure? She didn't know where to start. In this moment she felt complete. As though a huge part of her had been missing and she'd just found the last puzzle piece. She placed her hands on his muscular backside, relishing the way he flexed and tensed as he moved inside her. With each thrust building and building to a cataclysmic conclusion. She'd thought that her last orgasm had ruined her. This? She feared it would be world-ending. She was so open, vulnerable. The way they were joined was unlike anything she'd dreamed. He kissed her, lush and deep. Tongues moving in time to their own unique rhythm. Losing themselves till Lena was nothing but a mass of nerve endings pulsing with the anticipated pleasure of release. Then a burn started deep inside. Curling, twisting, tighter, as she raced towards the inevitability.

'Lena, I'm going to…'

Gabe's voice drifted off as their movements changed. Harder. Faster, as if running a race. Then less co-ordinated.

'Gabe!'

He moaned. 'You've ended me.' Thrusting into her one last time before stilling.

Something inside her snapped free. The ecstasy of letting go. Being cut adrift. Lena held on to Gabe tight as she fell and fell. Knowing that nothing would ever be the same again.

CHAPTER SEVEN

LENA AWOKE TO the first sounds of birdsong. She snuggled
into the warmth of the bed, wondering why she was awake
so early. The sun hadn't yet risen, everything lay dark outside. She should still be fast asleep, after a night of lovemaking with Gabe. Perhaps it was that they'd planned to wake
earlier than normal, so she could leave for her own room
without being seen, though she still had plenty of time before the house began to stir.

Her phone pinged with a message. That had to be the
reason. Usually she turned off her alerts at night so she
wouldn't be disturbed. She'd forgotten last night, because
she'd been otherwise…occupied. Lena smiled. Heat drizzled
over her at the memories, like being immersed in a warm
bath. The all-consuming pleasure she'd experienced. How
she'd felt seen, desired, *wanted*. Gabriel stirred beside her,
rolled over, still asleep. Even in the darkness of early morning his face was peaceful, hair flopped over his forehead in
a boyish kind of way.

She grabbed her phone and turned the volume down so
as not to wake him. Checked the time and almost groaned.
Four. Ugh. Not fair. Another alert came in. Silent this time.
That was unusual. After their conversation yesterday, she

was worried it was her mother or brother. She opened her notifications and saw a stream of them.

Her heart picked up its beat. She swallowed. What was wrong? She went to the texts first. None from her mother, thank goodness. That was a problem for another day. But there were a few from Gabe's private secretary, Henri.

Have you looked at your post?

Did he mean the video? And why would he be awake now after hitting the clubs last night? Of course, he'd looked as though he'd wanted to party. Maybe he was *still* out? It didn't matter now.

She decided she'd check the alerts she'd set up for Gabe first, opening her email. A number of newspaper headlines popped up. Lena began to read.

'Oh,' she said softly.

Gabriel stirred again, and his eyes blinked open. When he saw her awake he gave her a wicked smile, full of intent, that made her toes curl.

'Good morning,' he murmured, his voice gravelly and rough. 'Why are you awake?'

'Forgot to turn off my phone notifications and they've been…something.'

'Problem?'

'No… I don't think so.'

'Then what is it?' he pressed.

'Oh, just Henri getting in touch with me…'

He snorted. 'Your job never sleeps. Neither do you, apparently. I obviously didn't do my own job well enough last night.'

'You did a superlative job last night.'

Gabriel settled his hand on her leg. His fingers tracing a distracting circle on her inner thigh.

'Then why are you looking at your phone right now?'

'Henri suggested it might be a good idea.'

'That *does* sound like a problem.'

'Not really. The press picked up my football post.'

The article showed stills from her video. The headline *From Throne to Field: Prince Gabriel's viral kick proves he's still got it.*

Gabriel let out a heavy sigh. 'What do they say?'

'Um…this one says you've still got it.'

Gabe snorted.

'I feel affronted. I didn't think I'd ever lost *it*.' He then gave her a slow smile, one that might be described as panty-melting, had she been wearing any. 'What would you say?'

She smiled right back. 'I wouldn't presume to make any assumptions, Your Highness.'

'Are you going to put down that phone now? I can think of some ways that might help us get back to sleep for another hour. Or, if you don't want to go back to sleep, ways that might be able to make us very happy for a while.'

'I just need to finish…' She waved her phone at him.

'You're detrimental to my ego. If you didn't read between the lines, I'm offering to make love to you. That you're not jumping at the opportunity is leaving me suitably chastened.'

'I think what I'm doing right now might help your ego.'

Lena scrolled through the video she'd posted. Hundreds of thousands of views. Thousands of comments. Another text from Henri, saying the international press were getting in touch.

'All I can say is, it might be good we're going home this afternoon. You don't have much on by way of official duties this morning, apart from the planting?'

It was a final farewell at the palace, where Gabe was to plant a tree to signify the enduring ties between Halrovia and Lauritania.

'No.'

'Well, I think the press might want to ask you some questions.'

'About what? Me kicking a ball?' Gabriel asked.

'With respect, you did a bit more than just kick a ball.'

She showed him the post. The numbers of views and comments climbing and climbing.

'You did say you were happy to go viral,' she said, a little breathless. She'd done well before, but never achieved anything like this.

'I'm guessing we've achieved it.'

Lena liked that he saw them as a team. For the first time in a long time, she truly felt part of something. She nodded as he lay back, hands behind his head, something like a smug smile on his face. She'd never seen that expression before. Gabriel seeming so…satisfied with himself. It was a good look on him.

'Oh, no, they're at it again,' she said.

'Who?'

'People are saying you're a thirst trap.'

'A what?' Gabe looked bemused for a moment. Shook his head. 'Don't worry. No need to explain it.'

Gabriel's phone began to ping as well.

'Why are people not asleep? Why are we not asleep? Or,

even better, doing something entirely more enjoyable?' he said, reaching for his phone.

She noticed he didn't grab his glasses. In fact, she realised she'd never actually seen him in glasses before. Or really reading much at all.

'What does Cilla want?' Gabe muttered. 'And why is *she* awake right now?'

Gabe opened the text, and his phone read it aloud to him.

OMG Gabe. Exclamation mark. His Royal Hotness. I told you Lena's the best. Exclamation mark. Call me when you're awake.

That was strange. Why would he want his phone to read out a message?

Gabe took a deep breath in. Let a slow breath out.

'Did they really call me His Royal Hotness?' he asked, incredulous.

'Yes,' Lena said, sitting up. Looking down at him. Something niggling at her.

Gabriel began to chuckle, then laugh. 'None of this is real. It's ridiculous.'

'Your phone. It read that text message to you,' she said. 'Is that what you do when you don't have your glasses? Is your sight that bad?'

She found it hard to believe. He did most things without issue. Kicked a ball into the back of a net just fine. Maybe it was just a problem with reading and not long distance... Except Gabe had suddenly stopped laughing, as if the sound had been cut off. He sat up himself. Scrubbed his hands over his face. His palms scratching over his morning stubble. He put down his own phone. Took her hands in his. Looked at her. His face serious.

'My phone reads my messages because I have trouble reading them. I have dyslexia.'

Gabe didn't know why he revealed it at this point, only that he wanted honesty, because she'd been honest with him the night before. She'd told him about her virginity when she hadn't needed to say anything at all. And this morning she'd asked. He wouldn't lie. Not to her.

'Who knows?' Lena asked.

'My family. Pieter. My private secretary…'

She dropped her head, looked at where their hands were joined.

'So, the glasses?'

'I'm sorry,' he said. Meaning it. 'Not real. They have plain glass, not prescription lenses. They're a ruse. A deflection.'

'And your earbuds. Do you listen to music?'

'Occasionally. Mainly they're for listening to documents. I have a screen reader too.'

His heart rate kicked up a notch. What did she think of him on learning this? That he'd kept it hidden from her. He remembered when the word was first mentioned to his parents. Their thin-lipped, stony expressions. Yet he didn't see that with her…

Lena frowned. 'Do you have any ability to…?'

'Yes. But it takes time. When I'm stressed, or trying to do things in a hurry, it's not as easy for me. I use aids to simplify things.'

She pulled her hands away from his. Put her phone on

the bedside table. He felt as though there was a distance growing between them and he craved the closeness again. Lena fixed him with her assessing gaze. Cocked her head.

'Why haven't you told anyone?'

Wasn't that the question? His parents had been the ones who thought it should be kept quiet. That people might wonder about his ability to rule, given he was still quite young with no track record. They had claimed it might cause unnecessary concern to the Halrovian people. Even though the doctor said there were numerous scions of business with the condition. Then his ex-girlfriend had happened, and the secrecy over his diagnosis had seemed to increase.

He'd wondered, much later, whether one of the real reasons was it would ruin the illusion of their family's perfection...

'I was diagnosed quite late. In my teens. People thought I was lazy at school. It turns out that wasn't the issue at all. Back then it was the decision of my parents and their advisors.'

Lena reached out and placed her hand on his forearm. Squeezed. He relished that small touch. 'This is exactly the kind of authenticity people want to see from you. Why did your parents hide it? Were they ashamed?'

He shook his head in vehement denial, even though a kind of uncertainty pricked inside him.

'No. Not ashamed...' Though they'd never really said anything much. Were they embarrassed? It was a reasonable explanation for why they didn't want him studying. Then there was the question of why they'd wanted his diagnosis buried so deeply. Deeply enough to give a manipulative, untrustworthy man a position of advisor of state, to keep his daughter quiet. 'They believed I should establish myself in my role, show I could "do the job", so to speak. Then it became something we never really talked about.'

'It's something you could talk about now. People would relate. Don't you see?'

'It doesn't seem relevant…' He had trouble understanding what difference it would make. That was in the past. Behind him. He'd found ways of adapting. Moving forwards. He still did everything expected of him. He had no limitations. He'd proven it hadn't affected him at all. There wasn't any reason to say anything any more.

'Gabe, is this why you're always holding back from people? Accused by the press of being "proper". Because you're afraid people will find out the truth?'

The comment hit straight to the heart of him. She left no prisoners.

'I'm not afraid.' He'd reorganised his life around his dyslexia, had reading aids when he needed them. These things made life easier, for him and his staff. There was no part of the job that was beyond him, no impact on his role. Telling everyone now…at the mere thought, pressure in his chest grew.

Yet Lena wasn't judging him. She looked at him, not with pity, but with softness and concern. All he saw was care and understanding, not disapproval. What he would have given to see that expression on his parents' faces when he'd received his diagnosis. He hadn't realised for how long he'd craved simple compassion and acceptance. Here it was being shown to him by this beautiful, insightful woman. That increasingly relentless pressure in his chest began to ease.

'Telling everyone might help other people. Those subjects who are just like you.'

Her words jolted him back into the harshness of reality. How would he even begin to admit what he'd kept quiet for so many years?

'Imagine the charities you could support,' she said.

Before her marriage, his sister Ana's favoured charity was one for child and adult literacy. He'd never stopped to question whether she chose it as silent support for him. It hadn't crossed his mind. When she'd left to marry, her royal Halrovian patronages had fallen vacant. They'd need to be redistributed. Perhaps he could talk to his parents about it? Show them it made sense. It was something to think about.

But for now, all he wanted to think about was Lena. Sitting up in bed, hair an unruly tousle after their night of lovemaking. Mascara smudged under her eyes. Making them look smoky, sultry. Her lips a deep cherry red, well kissed.

If he'd been sensible, he would have called the kitchens to make coffee, then let her go. She'd called it the evening before. One night. Yet, seeing her in his bed, Gabriel knew he didn't want this to stop. Last night had been like nothing he'd ever experienced. The passion. The need. Sex with anyone else was a distant, faded memory next to her.

He knew there were ground rules for this sort of thing. Lena didn't come from this world. She mightn't understand that if this went on there could be no hint of anything between them. That nothing about their situation could be considered normal. It wasn't fair to her, yet he didn't want to give her up. Not yet. He was sure they'd burn out eventually. Once they'd glutted on each other's bodies. They'd both become bored of each other, and it would end. But for now...

As if she knew he was staring at her, contemplating their short-term future, Lena looked up at him. 'What?'

Something must have shown on his face. 'I've been thinking.'

'Indeed.' The corner of her mouth kicked up. She'd sounded so much like him in that moment. The same imperious tone he knew he could inject into his voice. Often did, deliberately. Of course, she knew it too. 'Are you going to suggest some wardrobe changes for me that I might reject?'

There was that gentle teasing again. He enjoyed it, how natural she was. How he'd come to believe that she *saw* him. Not for what he was, but for who.

'Wardrobe? I'd have you permanently naked if I could.' He growled at the crime of ever putting clothes on her magnificent body.

'I don't know how I'd get anything done.'

'You wouldn't. But that's not what I want to discuss. This. Us. I don't want to let it go. Not yet...' he said, wondering how he could canvass the rest. 'However—'

'It needs to be kept private.'

He wasn't sure whether she was reciting what she'd assumed he was going to tell her or setting her own rules. Whatever the reason, relief flooded over him that they were both on the same page.

'I want to protect you. From any claims that you're doing this to further your career, which I know you're not, because the results speak for themselves. Also, from the press. They can be cruel to me, *never* to you.'

'I know they'd flay someone like me alive.'

Someone like her? He wasn't sure what that meant and

he didn't like that she was okay with thinking that she was in some way less.

'I don't want you mobbed whenever you're out.'

'You're the story, Gabriel. I've never wanted the limelight.'

He didn't really want it either. 'Sadly it comes with being me. If I weren't a prince—'

'You'd be an international football player, and still famous.'

She showed such uncompromising faith in him. When had he *ever* had that before? 'Perhaps.'

Lena chewed on her lower lip, a look of uncertainty there. He wanted to kiss it away. 'How would it even work? I can't just stroll up to your apartments. People would get suspicious.'

'I have a way. Trust me. No one will know. Your reputation will be safe.'

'Don't keep me waiting.'

He smiled. She was going to agree? His heart pumped hard and fast. His desire once again roaring to life with a need like he'd never experienced before. Luckily, he'd texted his staff the night before, arranging a later start than usual. He could make love to her again before she had to go back to her room. Go back to pretending, till the next time at least.

'If I promise we won't be found out, will you agree?'

'Yes,' she said with a little smile. 'Yes, I will.'

He wanted to grab her, kiss her senseless, but he also liked the game they played. The fun. The banter. All part of the seduction.

'So,' he said, intent on changing the subject so they wouldn't have to waste any more time. 'His Royal Hotness?'

'You forget. Hashtag His Royal Hotness. Hashtag thirst-trap,' she replied.

'Do you think I'm hot?'

As the sun began to hint over the horizon, a pretty blush crept up her chest. Higher. Her ears turning a soft shade of pink.

'If the hashtag fits.' A teasing smile crept onto her face. 'There was another one. Bend it like Gabriel. What does that mean?'

'It's a football term. I can show you what it means later, but do you know what I'd like to do now?'

'No, Your Hotness—I mean, Highness.'

He loved the irreverence in her tone.

'I'd like to bend you over the bed. Make love to you till you scream as the sun rises.'

Lena squealed, giggling as he wrestled her into delicious submission. Covering her with his body.

'Let me show you just how hot I am,' he growled into her ear as she relaxed underneath him. Arms curling round his neck. Threading into his hair as Lena smiled at him.

'I look forward to you living up to the promise of your online reputation.'

CHAPTER EIGHT

LENA SAT IN her room, her heart beating as fast and light as a butterfly's wing. It had been a few days since they'd returned from Lauritania. Apart from during their workdays, she hadn't seen anything of Gabriel after hours, as he'd had meetings and dinners, making it impossible. Yet he'd promised her there was a way and, today, she'd received a text from him:

Wait for me in your room tonight. Seven thirty. Wear flat shoes. Don't eat.

So here she was, waiting as he'd asked. She wanted to get up, pace—impatient, nervous, excited all at the same time. How were they going to do this? She'd asked for one night because that was all she'd expected. Losing her virginity and moving on. Yet the hunger. It was a compulsion impossible to ignore. Beyond mere desire, a need. She'd never expected to experience this with a man, even more, a *prince*. What would it be like to have someone actually fall in love with her? To marry? Gabe. Someone so far above her…

No. That wasn't what their agreement was. As for his status, she'd come to think of them as equals. He was funny, self-deprecating, with a wry sense of humour. He didn't seem to take himself too seriously, even though there were serious parts to his role. She felt privileged to see this side of him. The side she wanted to show to the world: the man, not the prince. But Lena had no idea how he thought they could do this secretly. Though Gabe had *promised*, and she believed him. It was an intoxicating thing, to be able to simply believe in someone. That they'd have your interests at heart, as well as their own…

Lena checked the time on her phone. Seven twenty-eight. It heightened the anticipation that she had no idea *what* she was waiting for. She amused herself with a fantasy that he'd rappel down the walls and sneak in her window, or wear some disguise to turn up at her door, all the while realising those imaginings were fanciful and ridiculous.

The time ticked over. Seven thirty. She stood and walked to the window. The sun had dipped below the horizon now, the lights twinkling in the city below them.

'Lena.'

A male voice. She squeaked, unable to help herself, whipping around, and there he was, standing in her room.

Gabe.

She wanted to run to him, fling her arms about his neck, but that wasn't the kind of relationship they had…some teenage fantasy. This was all grown up. Lena held herself back and, instead, admired him. He wasn't in a suit tonight. Dressed more casually, in tan trousers, an open-necked shirt, no jacket, no tie. His hair still slightly damp, roughly dried. So handsome, it took her breath away.

'How did you get in here without me hearing you?'

The corner of his mouth kicked up. 'This palace has many secrets, and I know them all. Ready?'

'Of course. But where are we going? And how?'

'To my room,' he said with a sly grin. 'Follow me.'

He walked through into her bedroom. She was happy she'd made her bed and that it wasn't a mess, though she'd brought few belongings with her, as she hadn't known how long she'd be staying given he'd initially placed her on probation. Now she guessed she should get more of her possessions sent from home since she was staying...

As his PR and image consultant, of course.

Gabe walked up to the wall next to her bedside table, to a panel where there was a beautiful embossed rose detail she'd admired when she'd first moved in here. He pressed, and the panel swung inwards.

'You're kidding,' she said.

Gabe winked, making her toes curl. 'Secret passageways. My sisters and I used to play in them when we were children. We were terrors, visiting each other's rooms when we should have been sleeping. In the end my parents had the doors in our rooms barricaded with large furniture to stop us exploring. But that didn't stop me. Many places in this palace are interconnected. How did you think I was going to get to your room?'

'I don't know. I was imagining all kinds of things, like a disguise or you rappelling down the side of the palace to my window.'

He chuckled. 'No theatrics or daring, I'm afraid.'

'This seems pretty daring to me.'

'Up for an adventure, then?'

She nodded.

'After you.'

He motioned with his hand and she walked through into the dark, unlit space behind her walls. He followed as she waited just inside the passageway.

'But first,' he said, easing her up against the wall in the semi-darkness. The rough stone cool against her back. The only light coming from her room. Gabe cupped her cheek. 'You look so beautiful. These past few days have been *torture*, unable to touch you. Kiss you.'

He dropped his lips to hers. Hard. Unforgiving. Desperate. She matched him. Slipping her hands into his hair. Holding him close. Never wanting to let him go, although that was just for now, not for ever. The ache at that thought fled as they reacquainted themselves with each other's bodies. Touching. Teasing. How long they stayed there, she couldn't say. Time lost all meaning. All she knew was that when they pulled apart, she was overheated, and they were both panting.

'We need to go or I'll take you up against this wall.'

'I don't mind the sound of that.'

Gabe chuckled and the sound echoed in the cavernous space. 'Noted, for another time.'

He bent down and picked up something off the floor. There was a muffled click, and a beam of light from a torch illuminated the space with a cool glow. Gabe walked to the open panel in her wall and closed it shut. Shut them in.

'Where does this lead?' she whispered.

Gabe reached out his hand, and she took it. Threading her fingers through his. He squeezed.

'To many places, including my apartments. It was lucky that your room connected to mine.'

They began walking, their footsteps echoing around them.

'How do you find your way?' Her voice was a hiss in the darkness.

'I learned exploring as a child. There are also plans. However I have a pretty good mental map of the place.'

'Does anyone else use these?' she asked as they walked through. The air was a little stuffy, warm.

'Our personal staff, rarely. Kitchen staff, when we have large functions, because there's a passage that leads into the ballroom, but most of the time they sit unused. I still walk through if I want a shortcut. I've made some marks should you want to come back to your room on your own. If you want to find mine.' He shone the torch onto the walls and Lena saw arrows in chalk. Gabe squeezed her hand again. She squeezed back.

'Very resourceful,' she said, still keeping her voice low, quiet.

'I'm not just a…what did you call me. Thirst trap?'

'That's your hashtag. Why am I whispering?' she asked.

'I don't know. No one can hear us here. It's quite safe.'

She looked at the wall again, with the chalk-marked arrows. Small but clear. All pointing to her room.

'How do I get back in?'

'I'll show you when we get to my end. There's a small latch. It's easy. The only problem is when there's furniture across the doorway. People have forgotten these passageways, or deliberately blocked them off. I can only imagine what would have been done using them,' he said, chuckling.

'A little like what we're doing now.'

'I have no doubt.'

Gabe seemed to pick up the pace. She followed his purposeful stride. 'How long will it take?'

'Shorter than walking through the hallways to get to my room, since I'm in another wing entirely,' he said. 'You're not afraid?'

'No, it's amazing! I've always wanted to walk through a secret passageway. Think of the things you could do!'

'I suspect they were used for espionage. Invite foreign dignitaries to stay, put them in the right quarters, and then you could stand in these passageways and listen.'

'Really? I would have thought the walls were too thick.'

'In certain places there are what appear to be air vents in the walls. They're not. They're listening ports.'

'Oh, that's very underhanded of you and your family. Would they be used now?'

He shook his head. 'We prefer diplomacy rather than subterfuge.'

'Isn't subterfuge what we're doing?'

Gabe chuckled again. 'I suppose it is. Must be in my blood.'

Or hers...but she didn't want to dwell. Gabe didn't have another family stashed away. They were both single, free to do whatever they wanted. She tried not to think about how they were sneaking about secret passageways to see each other. What that meant.

After a few more minutes Gabe slowed, stopped. Shone the torch on the wall, illuminating an X in chalk.

'X marks the spot,' she said. 'These are your rooms?'

'Yes. Pieter has the night off, so we won't be disturbed. Here's the mechanism to get in.' There was a complicated-looking lever in the wall. He depressed it, then turned, and the door snicked open. He closed it again.

'You try.'

She did. Once he appeared satisfied that she could get into his room from the passageway, he pulled on the handle and led her through, closing the door behind them.

Lena walked into what appeared to be a dressing room with racks of suits, business shirts—all perfectly ordered. No surprises there. It seemed as neatly ordered as himself. The space was imbued with that scent of him. Woodsy. Green. Fresh, like the cool mountain air. She breathed him in.

'Come this way,' he said, placing his hand on her lower back, the warmth of his fingers seeping into her skin as he led her into a lounge area. The light from some side lamps painting the room in gold. Glorious silks lined the walls. The furniture sumptuous, comfortable-looking, yet undoubtedly antique. An elegant room she could see he fitted into, and clearly the room of Halrovia's prince.

But what struck her aside from the opulence was something else. All around the room, all surfaces had candle holders and candles, imbuing the space with a warm, flickering light. In the corner, by what appeared to be a set of windows with the curtains drawn, was a beautiful little table with armchairs. On the table flickered small tea-light candles in holders. There was a bunch of flowers in a cut-crystal glass that glittered in the low light. Beside the table was a wine bucket, wine on ice.

Gabe stood behind her, hands on her shoulders. His body warm against hers. He leaned down, his breath brushing her ear. 'Do you like it?'

'I love it,' she said. Tears prickled her eyes at the time and care this would have taken, the organisation. She turned. 'How did you manage to do all of this without anyone finding out?'

He smiled.

'It's easy. I know where the palace stores are. It wasn't hard to get supplies. The flowers are from my terrace outside. I have a small kitchenette area if I ever want a snack without calling the chef late at night.'

'It's thoughtful. Beautiful...' Romantic, even though this wasn't a romance.

'But it's not as beautiful as you,' he said, sliding his arms around her waist. Kissing her gently this time. Long, deep and slow. She closed her eyes, relishing the attention. The care he'd taken. How would she live without this when it ended? All she'd expected was mind-altering passion. This was something else entirely.

Gabe finally pulled away and all Lena wanted to do was grab him and drag him right down again.

'We need to stop or we'll never get to eat. Come to the table,' he said, leading her over and pulling out her chair as she sat. He then went to a sideboard, opened it, and retrieved a small plate.

'The food's a little simple tonight. I said I was hungry so they'd give me more, but asked for something light that I could snack on. I hope there's something here that suits. Help yourself.'

He kept the smaller plate for himself and gave her the gold-embossed royal dinner service and cutlery. There were cured meats, cheeses, small salads, pickles, then a little cooked food. Potato rösti, some sausages. Bread with pats of butter, embossed with the royal seal. She helped herself, her stomach growling.

'Next time I shouldn't leave you so long. Would you like wine?'

She nodded, biting into a crispy rösti. It was a little cool but still delicious. Gabe uncorked and opened the wine. Poured the pale fluid into her glass and his own before raising it.

'To subterfuge.'

Lena raised her glass, touching it to his. 'To secret passageways.'

She took a sip of the crisp, fresh wine. Trying to ignore the niggle in the back of her mind that this was not where she saw her life leading. She didn't want to ruin tonight, not after the effort Gabe had gone to. Tomorrow she could give this strange feeling more thought. Instead, she'd savour the delicious food. The sight of Gabe, relaxed. Happy in front of her. Lena changed the subject, to safer ground.

'It seems one of the men who played football with you must have sold a picture of you to the press.'

Gabe's eyebrows raised. 'Good on him, if he can get some money for it. Which one was it?'

She reached into the pocket of her dress, pulled out her phone. Showed him. To her shame she'd screenshotted it. It was the moment Gabe had winked at her. He'd seemed so alive, full of movement and passion.

The look on his face…as if he'd just rediscovered himself. She showed him.

'That's hardly interesting.'

'The press are applauding your new look, an image makeover.'

'Yet nothing's changed at all. I didn't even have to wear a mohair coat to achieve it.'

Something *had* changed though. Them. She ignored the

bruised kind of feeling his comment inflicted. It's all part of how they were together. Flirtatious. Fun. Not serious. With a definite 'use by' date, even though the end date hadn't really been specified. Though what would it be like to be *chosen* for once. Enthusiastically. Openly…

They were thoughts for another time, when the possibilities were real. Not this glorious fantasy.

'You'll never let me live that coat down.'

He shook his head. 'Probably not, no.'

'It was only to show you possibilities. Anyway, here you are, almost casual.' She waved her hand in his general direction. 'You're not even wearing a tie. What would the King and Queen's private secretary say?'

'I don't give a damn about him,' he growled, almost feral. A delicious shiver ran through her at the sound. 'I only care what you think.'

Gabe fixed her with his pale blue gaze. Once she'd thought it frigid. Now she couldn't miss the heat shimmering from the depths of him. He was like a frozen lake. Cool on top, with a whole world teeming underneath the icy surface.

She placed her phone on the table. As she did, a message came in from her brother. Lena's heart rate spiked.

'You're frowning.'

'I… Do you mind if I look at this? It's my family.'

'Of course,' Gabe said, his face warm with concern.

She opened the message, saying that her mother wasn't coping with the idea of a move. She texted back, repeating that she'd fix it but for now they'd need to find somewhere else to live. There were no other options. Lena took a deep breath. Any properties her mother had suggested were the same rent or even more expensive than where they lived right now. She couldn't understand the abject denial of reality. She never wanted to be like that. Pretending everything was okay. That life didn't have to change when it so clearly did. Lena turned her phone over so she couldn't see any other messages. Tried to eat some of her meal, but it tasted like ash.

Gabe reached out and placed his hand over hers. 'Everything okay?'

She desperately wanted to say something. For most of her life, there'd been nothing she could admit about her family. So much had had to be kept secret. Her friendships were affected by it. Her life had been bound by the silence. Her mother always choosing her father's need for secrecy. What would it be like to share something of what she had to go through—the burden she carried?

Gabe had shared his dyslexia with her. He'd been honest. He'd trusted her, so surely she could trust him? She had spent so long hiding her father's identity that it was difficult to let that go. But perhaps she could give a little.

'My mother has to move out of her home. She isn't coping well with the idea.'

Gabe frowned. 'Why does she have to go anywhere?'

What could she say that didn't leave her family exposed? 'My mother and father weren't together, but he still supported the family. My brother's studying and, whilst he's on a partial scholarship, it still costs money. When my father died…'

Gabe stroked his thumb gently over the back of her hand. It was such a comfort that he just sat. Listened.

'He left no provision in his will. I had to stop studying

myself. Things have been a little…tight, and now the land-lord has put up my mother's rent. I've told her she has to go somewhere smaller. Within our budget.'

'Do you need—?'

'No, everything's fine.' Lena feared Gabe was going to offer money and she couldn't take anything from him. It felt too much like crossing a line that she wouldn't be able to walk back from. 'It's just difficult for her because she's lived there for so long. But the place is too big, what with me no longer there. She needs to downsize.'

'Does she? Surely if she needs support succession laws would give her some protection?'

What could Lena say to that other than a phrase that car-ried a multitude of possible answers.

'It's complicated.'

Something about Gabriel's gaze darkened. 'What fami-lies aren't? Are you sure there's nothing I can do? Ask some lawyers—'

'No, thank you. As I said, we'll be fine. It's just… I might need some time off work to go and help her sort it out. Maybe find somewhere else to live, show her that it'll be all right. My brother isn't as good at reassuring her as I am.'

'Of course,' Gabriel said. 'Take any time you need.'

'I'm sorry. I've only been in the role less than a month.'

'As I've said before, I look after my valued employees.' Something about the use of that word when it came to her seemed like a sharp spike to the heart. But she was what she was. They couldn't deny their respective positions.

'We have generous leave plans here. This is a family emergency. Any time will be covered.'

'Gabe, thank you. I don't know what to say.'

'There's nothing *to* say. Only promise me. If you need anything…'

Gabriel stood, held out his hand. She placed hers in it and stood too. He wrapped his arms around her and held her close, held her safe. It was the first time in so long that she'd felt as though anyone cared for her. That there might be someone who'd look after her, worry about her, who might *love* her.

No, not love. She'd seen what love had done to her mother. It was a trap that led to poor choices. She'd never succumb to the same thing. Something inside her stilled, gave her pause. Wasn't that what she was doing here? Gabe was unavailable…

No. She didn't have to think about it now. She'd go back to Isolobello, figure out her family's problems and then think about herself. Her aim had always been to secure her future and her finances first and then, maybe, consider a man in her life. Even though the idea of another man left a sour sensation in her gut. She was a loyal person, that was all. Lena didn't believe in cheating. She allowed herself this, Gabriel's tenderness. Because it was nice to know there was someone who might think about her, who seemed to care.

For a few moments, she just rested her head on his chest. Listening to the solid sound of his heartbeat as he cradled her in his arms. Letting her tears silently fall. Lena realised she'd never really cried about this before. She'd spent her whole life trying to rein in her emotions, so nobody could hurt her. She wanted to be soft and vulnerable, just for a little while. She owed herself that much.

She drew in a shuddering breath. Gabe pulled back. Lena tried to look down at the floor so he wouldn't see her tears. He placed his fingers gently under her chin and tilted her head up.

'Lena,' he murmured, his voice full of concern. 'Do you want any more to eat?'

She shook her head. Wiped her face. 'Why do I always seem to cry around you?'

'I wish you were crying because of pleasure, not pain.'

A kindle of heat ignited at her core. She didn't want to talk. She didn't want looks of pity or sympathy. He was right. He could give her something else. Pleasure sounded good. Pleasure could wipe away the pain, the fear. It was what she wanted more than anything in this moment—to simply forget.

'You'd prefer to see me with tears of pleasure rather than pain? Then there's something you can do about that,' Lena said, stepping in close to him once more. Placing her hand on his chest. 'I want you to take me to bed.'

'I want you to take me to bed.'

Lena's tears of sadness almost broke him. He couldn't bear to see her like this, yet he knew what her request was all about—avoidance. Hadn't he buried himself in a warm, willing body more than once in the past, trying to forget things in his own life? But this was different. Something about *her* was different. Whilst he could happily give Lena exactly what she craved right now, he wanted to make sure it was the right thing for her.

He knew that he could bring a look of ecstasy to her face. That he could make her forget everything that caused this sadness. Maybe it really didn't matter, allowing Lena to run away from her problems for a little while. He could do that for her, then maybe she wouldn't mind him exploring legal options with his lawyers, to see if there was any way of getting money for the family to which they had to be entitled, given her father had still been supporting them when he died. There *must* be some bequest for them, no matter how 'complicated' things were.

'I'm happy to take you to bed and make love to you till everything but us is forgotten. But I want to be sure that it's the right thing for you.'

'It's what I want. I want to forget for a little while, remember what it's like to feel alive.'

Yet somehow, it felt wrong. As if he wasn't solving any problem at all. There was a story there, and one day he'd get to the bottom of it. He had a terrible suspicion that she was holding something back from him. Still, she was entitled to her secrets in this affair they were having—though part of him rebelled at classing it as that.

Why did he feel as though that word cheapened everything, when what they had between them felt like so much more? Sure, there'd been no promises of a future, only a 'now'. He took a deep breath. 'Now' was all that he could give her, even though, in this moment, it didn't feel like enough. Still, she wanted him to pretend that everything was okay? If that was all she'd allow, that was the gift he'd grant her.

'Then come into my bedroom,' he said.

It was as if all the tension leached out of her. She seemed to slump a little before coming back into herself.

'Thank you.'

He hated that she thanked him as if he were doing her some favour. Later he'd question why she was like this. For now, he'd ratchet up the tension, play whatever game she needed to forget.

'You want me to make you scream?' he asked as she hurried after him.

'Yes.'

She stopped at the end of his bed. He couldn't wait to get her out of her dress. Tonight, a beautiful halter neck, patterned with what looked like peacock feathers. The fine fabric of her skirt drifting around her body.

'Undo the halter,' he commanded. Her pupils darkened and lips parted. She reached behind her neck and tugged. Her top fell free, exposing Lena's breasts, the perfect handful. Her skin a warm gold. He stalked forwards, cupped her breasts. Her nipples tight and dusky. Gabe stroked his thumbs over the diamond-hard peaks. So beautiful, irresistible. Her nipples tightened even further with his attention. He pinched them. Not too hard, just enough. Her eyelids fluttered shut and she moaned.

'I love how responsive you are, yet tonight, I demand silence,' he said as he kept up his ministrations. Teasing her pebbled flesh.

Her eyes flew open. 'What?'

She sounded almost drunk with desire. Lena wanted pleasure to make her forget? He'd heighten it a thousandfold.

'You might want to scream. What I want is quiet. You scream. I stop. You're silent, and I'll give you all the pleasure you need. Do you agree to my rules?'

He'd make her mindless with trying to comply. To fight her instincts. Of course he'd never leave her unsatisfied.

Even if she did scream, he wouldn't stop, although he might tease. But he looked forward to her attempts to hold everything in. How she'd break under his lips and hands.

She nodded. 'Yes.'

'Good.'

He stalked to the head of the bed, grabbed his pillows and propped them up against the bedhead before returning to her.

'Turn round,' he said. Lena did. Gabe traced a finger down her spine and goosebumps dusted her skin. He drew the zip of her dress down. It fell from her hips to the floor, leaving her only in fine lace panties. Gabe placed his palm on her belly. Drew her back to him so she could feel his hardness. How much he wanted her. Then he kissed the back of her neck, the side at the juncture of her shoulder, till she squirmed, pressing her backside against his body. Inflaming him. He gritted his teeth.

'Shoes off. On the bed propped up on the pillows.'

As she obeyed he turned off the lamps. He'd spent time decorating this room with candles as well. The soft light flickered, painting her in light and shadow.

Gabe slowly undid his shirt, tugged it out of his trousers. Cast it aside. Lena propped herself on her elbows, watching as he put on a show.

'Relax back,' he said as he came forwards onto the bed, sliding her panties down her legs. Dropping them on the floor. Her gaze looked almost out of focus, but she was now nestled deep into the down pillows, as he'd demanded.

He sat on the bed next to her, his hand tracing down her stomach, fingers slipping between her legs, which fell open at his touch.

'What's my rule again?'

'You want silence,' she whispered.

He smiled, kept stroking her. Lena's hips beginning to move in time with his rhythm. She was so wet. If he kept going much longer she'd come, he was sure of it.

'And what happens if you scream?'

'You stop.' Her voice was almost a whimper.

'That's right, but you won't scream, will you? You won't make any noise at all.'

She shook her head. He stopped touching her. Lena opened her mouth as if to object, then closed it again.

'I want you to watch what I'm doing to you,' he said.

He manoeuvred himself between her legs. Lay on the bed. Her eyes widened. 'Just lie back and enjoy.'

Her legs opened further to accommodate his shoulders as he propped himself on his forearms and dropped his head between her legs. Traced his tongue over her. The sweet salt, the scent of her arousal. He groaned. It would be a challenge to see who'd come last. He was so aroused, craving her orgasm almost as much as his own. He wanted her mindless, replete. Forgetting everything but his lips, tongue, hands. He didn't know if she watched—all his focus was on her pleasure. Her breaths came heavy and fast. Panting as he stroked her flesh with his tongue. Concentrating on her clitoris, the centre of her pleasure.

Her body trembled as she fought not to cry out. Her fingers gripping the coverlet till they blanched white. Gabe knew she needed more. He slid one finger inside, then another. Her legs shook, as if an earthquake were overtaking her body. Her back arching off the bed. His fingers slick with her arousal. He wasn't sure she was even breathing when he stopped the relentless rhythm of his tongue and sucked. She stilled. Stiffened, then broke in two. A high-pitched keening noise shattering the room. He didn't care. His plan had never been to deny her, but to give her every-thing. She pulsed around him as he waited for her to come down from her orgasm. Then he moved up to her. Lay on his back. Took her, lax and replete, into his arms.

Hoped, for a while, he'd allowed her to forget.

'It'll be fine, Lena,' he murmured. 'It'll all work out.'

As he said the words, Gabe wasn't sure whether he was talking about her family problems, or their time together.

CHAPTER NINE

HIS PALACE APARTMENTS felt stultifying after the freedom of his time away. Even though the building had seven hundred rooms and five apartments spread out over different wings, he still had this clawing sensation, as if he were trapped. He'd chosen his apartments to be at the opposite end from his parents and even that was too close. Nothing seemed to fit right now. His tie appeared too tight, the fine wool of his suits prickled. He was uncomfortable in everything he did. The only time he had a modicum of peace and felt he could truly *be* was with Lena. After a long day he'd let Pieter go for the evening, shut his door, and wait for the click of the secret door in his dressing room.

He and Lena would spend the evening over dinner, talking about the day. Their nights, making love. In the morning they'd wake early and Lena would leave. Then they'd start over again, to the world appearing as employer and employee until night fell and they could be lovers once more.

Only it was harder and harder to let her go as the sun rose each morning. Not reaching out to touch her in public. All things that had once seemed inconceivable, now as natural as breathing. Simple, yet impossibly complicated.

When he was with her, he wasn't thinking about a past or

a future, he simply *was*. Present in the moment. He started each day with enthusiasm, evident in the headlines that were to Lena's credit. It was clear she saw something he'd thought he'd lost. Showing the world as well.

He wasn't sure what he'd do when she left to take care of her family, even though that wouldn't be for ever. She'd come back. But...what if she didn't? Lise and Rafe had all but offered her a job. No doubt they'd pay a premium for her, and her family needed the money... Those thoughts made his chest tighten. No, she'd return. There was no question of it.

But what was she returning to? There'd been no promises between them, only short term with an uncertain end date. Once, that had seemed enough. To live firmly in the present with what they had, till things burned out between them. Where the future felt like something distant and unreachable. Except things didn't feel as though they were burning out. They were burning hotter.

He looked at himself in the mirror. The same face but, in so many ways, changed. Today he was opening a library. There, he knew he'd be asked to read a book to the children, but it didn't bother him any more. He'd practised reading it with Lena till the concern that he might stumble and forget something abated. All because she had a faith in him few others seemed to hold. Gabe wanted to sit with that realisation, what it meant, for him to have someone who was becoming so vital to him. What he needed was time, to sift through these complicated feelings running through him. To work out what they meant, because he'd never been in this position before.

Time was something he'd find, except this morning he

needed to button himself back into the role of Prince Gabriel, rather than Gabe Montroy. The man whose name Lena loved to scream to the room…

He shook his head with a wry smile to his reflection, then walked into the sitting room and grabbed his coffee, which he'd taken to leaving a little later in the morning given Lena's usual presence here. Nothing had been said, it was no one's business, but Gabe had the sense Pieter's normally cool demeanour had warmed a fraction. He took the time to relish the drink, before putting on a tie and getting the day started.

His valet walked into the room. 'Sir, may I suggest no tie today? Perhaps a more casual approach, for the children.'

'Are you falling under Ms Rosetti's influence?'

Pieter grinned. 'No, sir. She suggested a tie adorned with a popular cartoon character. That would never do.'

Gabe snorted. 'No. Perhaps not. What do the headlines say today?'

He could read them himself with less trouble now his stress had seemed to ease, a revelation that gave him hope things would improve even further. Something else to thank Lena for. Still, this was a routine with Pieter he enjoyed, particularly the way his valet read the headlines with such delicious disdain.

'I quite like this—'

A knock sounded at the door of his apartment, which immediately opened. His mother striding through. He gave her a quick bow, the visit unexpected.

She waved her hand at Pieter. 'You may leave us.'

The fact she tried to dismiss his staff rankled.

'Pieter was about to tell me what the headlines said.'

Pieter didn't move.

His mother walked to the coffee table, picked up one tabloid. Whilst Lena laughed that it was 'old school' not looking at the papers online, these habits were old ones.

'Ah, yes. *"Sisters Marry. Is Prince Gabriel Next? Speculation Grows as Nation Waits!"*'

'Hyperbole,' Gabe said. 'Cilla isn't married yet.'

'Priscilla will be married soon enough,' his mother said, ominously.

He was aware he'd need to marry some day. It was just that he never gave it much thought other than as a concept. He was thirty-two. There was no rush. His father was well. He had years to take the throne. Though a vision slammed into his consciousness, of Lena looking up at him, soft focus behind a veil… They were thoughts better had at another time. He filed them for later reference.

'Too many royal weddings too soon seems excessive.'

'Let's read another headline, shall we?'

His mother's tone was prickly, but then that tended to be her default, though she usually reserved her ire for her daughters, who had never lived up to her lofty expectations.

His mother's lips pursed as if she'd tasted something unpleasant. *"'From Eligible to Engaged? Prince Gabriel's New Look Fuels Bride Search Buzz!'"*

Gabe looked around and noticed that Pieter had quietly and sensibly slid from the room.

'Is there a point to your visit, Mother?'

'It seems that your makeover's working. Therefore, Miss Rosetti's services are no longer required. The role can be absorbed by others, using her formula for success.'

No!

The word shouted in his head. It was all he could do to keep quiet and not to shout the word *at* his mother. Lena's formula for success? She understood him. No one else could achieve the same because no one knew him as Lena did.

'*Others* have tried in the past, and they've failed. Lena stays.'

His mother grabbed another paper. Read it. Fixed him with her cold blue gaze.

'"*All Eyes on Prince Gabriel's Change: Is Love in the Air?*"'

His heart skipped a beat. Stilled. Why were they talking about love?

'The tabloid editors are being ridiculous. Royal weddings sell. Speculation about royal weddings sell even more.'

'Your father seems happy enough to allow this to continue. I know better.' His mother's voice was as cold as the first slap of a winter's wind across your face.

'I have no idea what you're talking about.'

'Save me the lies, Gabriel! You couldn't fool me when you were a child, and you don't fool me now. A dalliance is acceptable when the rules are followed.'

Gabe's blood froze. How could anyone know? They'd been careful. Whilst there was some element of protecting himself, he wanted to protect Lena from the vultures who'd descend. There was nothing wrong with what they were doing. They were two consenting adults. Whilst he'd once been sure it would burn itself out, he wasn't ready for it to stop now.

In fact, he wasn't sure he wanted it to stop at all.

'You have *no* rights to be having this conversation with me.'

'I'm *Queen*. I have every right. What's happening here is

plain. A change. A new look. Words about love on the front page? Tell me, Gabriel. What's brought about that change? You have *feelings* for the woman. Heaven save us from doe-eyed commoners who seek a station higher than their entitlements. She's your *employee*. What did we tell you? Stay within your circle, where everyone understands what's possible and what's impossible. Yet here we are. *Again.*'

A fire burned inside him. He wasn't some teenager who didn't know his own mind. He was the Crown Prince of Halrovia, the country's future, as Lena liked to remind him. Whilst Gabriel didn't want a war within his family, he'd demand to be treated like an adult. This remained no one's business other than his own. He didn't have to admit anything. Especially not to his parents.

'Your Majesty, I respect you as my mother but I'm an adult. Stay out of my business. My love life is my own. I will not be speaking about it with you. You're jumping at shadows whereas I'm here, settled in reality.'

In a reality where he no longer saw why he and Lena couldn't continue to see each other. This was supposed to be a modern monarchy. When Ana's engagement had been agreed, she'd simply left with her fiancé before they'd even set a wedding date. He'd been a commoner. Things like bloodlines didn't matter any more, not to Gabe, anyhow.

'The woman is a menace. What of her mother, her father? Do you know anything about them?'

'Conversations about parents are irrelevant. I enjoy Lena's company. Her professionalism and how she's acquitted herself are impeccable. I'm in no hurry to marry and, once again, I am an adult capable of managing my own life. You have no place there.'

His mother's lips narrowed as if preparing to spit out the next words.

'Did she tell you that her mother is said to be a notorious mistress, to a man who kept two households? One legitimate, one illegitimate. Who's to say Lena Rosetti isn't wanting the same from you? Her father's not named on her or her brother's birth certificate, yet the rumours abound about his identity. Did she tell you that as well? Lena Rosetti is unclaimed. She's a stray. And she is entirely unsuitable to be the partner of Halrovia's Crown Prince and next King.'

Lena froze in the front foyer of Gabriel's apartment. She'd forgotten her mobile when she'd left this morning and hadn't been thinking. She'd simply walked into his rooms without any care until…

Unclaimed? A stray? Entirely unsuitable?

She'd caught *everything*.

'Enough.' Gabe's voice was like she'd never heard before. Forceful. Cold, with a crack of anger. 'You will not speak of Lena, of *any* of my employees, like that ever again.'

She should leave immediately and yet remained frozen to the spot, wanting to listen to it all in some masochistic desire to hear Gabriel's responses. And yet when she had heard… The pain of it all knifed deep. He'd made it clear. No matter what they might have shared, she'd always been his employee.

What had she been thinking?

The truth was, she hadn't. It was all a blissful fantasy till reality invaded, because she wanted belonging. She wanted someone to want *her*. She wanted that man to be Gabe. Was that what had happened to her mother? Falling into a trap that she'd been unable to extricate herself from, wanting to feel wanted too? By a man as unavailable to her mother as Gabe was to her? She didn't know. But in this moment, Lena finally understood her mother a little better.

There was movement ahead of her and yet she was fixed to the spot. Not understanding why every word had been a knife to her heart. As though she were bleeding out here. There'd been no talk of a future between them. She and Gabriel had been living in the moment, hadn't they? But hearing it said out loud, *'I'm in no hurry to marry...'* made her finally face the truth, that maybe it was marriage she'd wanted all along. That she'd wanted Gabe, not for the short time they'd agreed, but *for ever.* Even if for ever hadn't been promised to her.

The Queen swept into the hall with Gabriel following, striding behind her. He cast Lena a brief glance, eyes widening for a second in surprise at her presence before a cold impassive demeanour slid over his face once more.

Any words choked in Lena's throat. She gave a quick curtsey as they passed, refusing to allow anyone to see her pain, holding it deep inside. Her Majesty didn't even deign to look at her. It was as if she simply didn't exist. Was that how her mother had always felt? Ignored? Invisible? She'd believed her only true parent had enjoyed her position, having been in it so long. Now Lena was coming to understand what might have held her mother in place, and what it had cost her.

Lena couldn't stay still now. She walked further into Gabe's apartment, found her phone. Not willing to face the Queen, or even Gabriel. She could slip out again, into the secret passageway that ran through the walls here, and melt away. When Gabe had first shown it to her, she'd thought it exciting. The thrill of walking through it from her own room in the employee's quarters, to his own. Heart pounding with every footstep as she got closer to the secret latch that opened a door into his rooms.

She'd imagined all kinds of things on those walks through the dimly lit corridors behind the walls. The thrill of two lovers, meeting in secret. Lena realised now that this was what had kept her going through the brutal walk back to her own room each morning. When all she wanted to do was to stay, not leave before daybreak and pretend until night fell again and the fantasy could begin once more. Because that was all it had been.

A fantasy.

Now, reality slapped her in the face. This hadn't simply been about 'living in the moment' or losing her virginity. She had feelings for Gabriel. She wanted *more*. Looking back, she probably always had.

'What did you hear?'

She gave a bitter laugh. 'Enough.'

Especially his mother's comments about her and her family. The ones that cut to her marrow.

'Is it true, about your parents?'

That was where he first went to? But of course. She was simply a commoner. One who'd done the unforgivable and fallen for a prince. She lifted her chin. Seeing things clearly now when she hadn't understood before. 'My mother's *only* sin was to love a man. My father's, such as he was, far greater. But they had a long relationship that lasted till he died. Most people can't say the same.'

'Why didn't you tell me?'

Part of her wanted to believe he sounded almost hurt that she hadn't disclosed the truth, but she refused to accept that he was experiencing that kind of emotion, after what she'd heard.

'Because it wasn't relevant. Because I didn't want any judgement imposed on either me, or my mother. Because I've had enough to last a *lifetime*.'

Because, Lena realised now, she could accept judgement from most people since they didn't matter. It would have crushed her if that sentiment had ever come from Gabe.

His eyes widened, yet he didn't seem chastened at all. He almost looked…pitying. She loathed pity in all its forms. She'd been pitied, disdained, for most of her life.

'*Lena*, I wouldn't have judged you, or your family.'

Perhaps that was right, but everyone else would have, and, no matter what might have happened between them, Prince Gabriel clearly didn't want her enough to have overcome it. He was a prince, and princes didn't choose people with indeterminate backgrounds like hers.

'I suppose you did say you enjoyed my company, and that my professionalism was impeccable. But I thought you might have…*liked* me, just a little.'

She hated how that statement showed her weakness. She'd wanted to be more than liked, she realised. She'd wanted to be loved. So *very* much. To be seen for who she truly was. Someone with a good heart who was interested in people. Who cared about showing the world the truth about a person, finding the good in those who were worthy, rather than mining the bad. She'd wanted to be seen as enough, even if she'd been kidding herself, because Gabe's view of her was built on a false picture. He'd never truly seen her because he didn't have the full truth. And she had no one to blame for that but herself.

'I do, like you. And there's no reason why this should change anything.'

She'd spent her whole short life trying not to be her mother's daughter, and yet here she was. Did her mother have these same conversations with her father? A public figure who could never truly be with her, so she'd had to accept whatever shreds of himself he'd deign to supply? Was that what Gabe would offer her too? That was not what she wanted. Lena shook her head. How couldn't he see?

'It changes *everything*.'

'Why? I understand this is your first physical relationship with a man so you might not realise that the chemistry we have is something rare. Something to be explored, not thrown away. My family has no part in what's happening between us.'

Yet again, there was no talk of feeling and, right now, her whole body was awash with it. The pain of what couldn't be. Because he might have wanted her for the physical side of their relationship, but he didn't want her for anything more. He was like every other man, who coveted what they saw physically, and didn't care for anything else. She could have laughed at how she hadn't listened to lessons that her life should have taught her. Self-deception sure was an intoxicating and potent drug.

'What if one of us decides they want something more?' Though she knew there was really no 'us' in this situation. The person who wanted more was her.

Gabriel frowned, but it was so hard to read him right

now she didn't know what it meant. Annoyance, frustration. She couldn't tell.

'I thought we were enjoying each other. If you're talking marriage, that's a long way off for me. I'm interested in now, which is what you said you wanted too. Time to think of futures much later.'

That might be okay if Gabriel were just any man. A commoner like her. But he wasn't. He was the Crown Prince of Halrovia. With duties and expectations imposed on him, that he'd willingly accepted. His commitment was what would make him such a good king when the time came.

'And what if one day you decided I was the woman for you? Can you imagine how it would impact your image? Because I can. Let's think up a headline…' Lena tapped her finger to her lips. '*The Prince's Shocking Romance! From Mistress's Daughter to Future Queen?* I bet it's something your family could write themselves.'

'I don't care about my image. I don't care about the headlines.'

He started forward, towards her, as if to take her in his arms. To comfort. But there was no way to make this better. She held her hand up in a stop motion. To his credit, Gabe didn't move a step further.

'Yes, you do. I was employed to help you fix them. You enjoyed it and you changed because of it. You *do* care. To say anything else is kidding yourself.'

Lena didn't want to be the one to destroy his image. She wanted to protect him. It wasn't just her background that was the problem, but the workplace romance too. Everything about this would see him judged, even though she'd been a willing party and in many ways the instigator of her own downfall. Well, she wouldn't be the cause of Gabriel's downfall as well.

'You need to listen to me.'

'No, I don't.' No matter what she agreed to, in the end he'd come to his senses and the story would be the same. One she was painfully familiar with. Gullible woman falls for high-profile, unavailable man.

'Our positions are clear. You broke some rules and so did I.'

'Good God, Lena.' Gabe raked his hands through his hair. 'I *care* about you.'

Like. Care. They were words, sure. Once they might have been enough. But they were bland now. Mere scraps thrown from a table of emotions when she wanted the whole banquet.

'My job's never been to make your life hard, Your Highness.'

Gabe's eyes widened. 'It's Gabriel, *not* Your Highness. I don't want easy. I don't need easy. Whatever rash decision you're about to make, the answer is no.'

As much as she needed to support her family, Lena needed to respect herself more. She knew the risks if she stayed. How easy it would be to be sucked back into the vortex that was Gabriel Montroy, dying a little each day because she was showing the man she loved to the world, and he could never choose her. Then what if he met the perfect princess bride? She'd be left as an unacknowledged footnote in his history. That was something she couldn't bear. 'You don't have a choice. There's no future here. There never was. One day you'll come to realise I was right, and you'll thank me for it. But it's time to go. I resign, Your Highness, effective immediately. Thank you for trusting me, when others might not have. Given I've exceeded your objectives, I look forward to my reference.'

Before he could say anything, Lena turned and strode out of his apartment. Walked away, before she could fling herself into his arms and beg him to love her. The tears burned in her eyes and she let them fall because doing the right thing was hard, and there was no shame in that. Lena loved Gabriel, but she loved herself even more.

And sometimes the best way to love was to let a person go.

CHAPTER TEN

GABRIEL HAD NEVER wanted to look back on his life with regret, but for one so relatively short—only thirty-two years—he'd had many. Yet none was greater than how he'd treated Lena. For days after she'd left, he'd been unable to forget the look on her face. The disappointment, as if something in her had shattered irreparably. The light in her snuffed out. What wounded almost beyond description was that *he'd* done it to her, hurt her. Not realising what he was about to lose because he hadn't thought to honestly look to the future. Mired, instead, in a past and present that no longer fitted the man he'd become.

It had taken Lena's loss to make him recognise how much she meant to him. Now it was as if he walked through a haze of apathy. Nothing held any interest. He was entirely unsure how to heal the pain he'd caused, to a woman who'd come to mean everything to him. Until he could, none of this meant anything at all.

'Are you convinced this is the right course, Your Highness?' his private secretary asked.

'It's the *only* course,' Gabriel replied.

There were few people he trusted implicitly. Henri. Pieter. His personal protection officers. Lena. But she wasn't here to give him advice any more. To share all the precious moments he might have once experienced, but hadn't properly valued until they were seen through the lens of her eyes.

His failure to protect her was like a knife to the gut. She was a woman with a tender soul. Someone who said what she thought without fear. A woman he'd craved to nurture, to protect. Yet the yawning ache in his chest called Gabriel out as a liar. He hadn't protected Lena at all, sneaking her through secret passages in the palace rather than proudly inviting her through the front door of his suite, forcing his parents to accept her.

He'd gone a little way to dealing with that issue in the brutal, bleak days after she'd walked out of his life. Gabe had spoken to the King and Queen and told them they needed to take a long, honest look at themselves. Suggesting the problems with the royal family's image were more likely due to the quiet disdain in which they appeared to hold those who weren't royal like themselves, rather than anything he or his siblings had done. Then he'd walked away from them, inviting communication between their respective private secretaries until they'd properly reflected on their actions, because in the time since Lena had walked away, a single truth had glared at him.

He might have a duty to his country, which he'd carry out willingly, but he didn't want it without Lena at his side.

If he couldn't have her, how could he perform the role? He'd be miserable, and he'd make a miserable king, which wouldn't be good for the country. He'd seen how his relationship with his people had changed since Lena had come into his life. It hadn't been the photographs, the curated view of himself, that had made the difference. It had been her. She'd demanded something honest from him—not the man in hiding, not the prince, but the *real* man.

He'd spent his whole life doing what was required of him, as opposed to what he might have truly desired. Yet duty could only take you so far. It didn't make you laugh. It didn't feed the soul. It didn't comfort or console, or keep you warm on a cold night. Lena was the one who'd offered him all those things. Encouraged him to contemplate more for himself. She'd held a mirror up to him and he finally saw himself through her eyes. That was the true gift she'd bestowed on him, recognition of the best parts of himself, the ones he'd tried to forget. That he was allowed to care but, even more, that he was allowed to show it. That he had dreams and aspirations that his people might want to see too.

Lena was the one who showed him.

Realising he was happy to walk away if it meant having her made his next task easier. He was tired of secrets. Those secrets, and a failure to address them, was what had led them here. To a place where his family was being held hostage by fear, and he was without the woman he loved. Because he'd come to realise, very soon after she'd resigned from her job and his life, that he was in love with Lena Rosetti. Now was his chance to be honest and, in some ways, atone for his personal failings.

He picked up the piece of paper that held a media release, drafted by him and his private secretary. Henri had loaded it into Gabriel's screen reader, but Gabe wanted to read the words on the page, to take the time and make the effort, since he'd written them because of Lena and in many ways *for* her. To show the woman he loved how he'd changed.

For immediate release:

His Royal Highness, Prince Gabriel of Halrovia, Adopts Patronage of Literacy Charity, sharing his personal journey with dyslexia to inspire and empower.

In a meaningful display of dedication to literacy and inclusivity, His Royal Highness, Prince Gabriel, has announced his new role as patron of the Halrovian Literacy Foundation, a charity dedicated to supporting children and adults in achieving reading confidence and fluency. In stepping into this patronage, His Royal Highness has also publicly shared his personal experience with dyslexia for the first time.

Since his diagnosis in his teens, Prince Gabriel has successfully learned to navigate the challenges dyslexia can present, allowing him to fulfil his royal duties and responsibilities. His diagnosis was kept private out of a belief that it was irrelevant to his public role. However, as he assumes leadership of the charity formerly championed by his sister, Princess Anastacia, he has chosen to share his story in the hopes of inspiring others facing similar challenges.

'Reading is something many take for granted but, for some, it's been a constant source of struggle and, occasionally, stigma,' Prince Gabriel said. 'My hope is that by sharing my story, others will feel less alone and more empowered to seek the help they need. With support and community acceptance of those with reading difficulties, we can all find ways to strive and thrive.'

With Prince Gabriel's support, the Halrovian Lit-

*eracy Foundation aims to reach even more people,
offering them the tools and encouragement to achieve
their personal best, supporting the Halrovian community's commitment to literacy and learning for all
its citizens.*

*Media Contact: Henri Lacoste, Private Secretary
to His Royal Highness, Office of the Crown Prince,
Halrovia*

Gabriel wished he'd had Lena's counsel before sending
the release, but she'd told him once that this was the kind of
authenticity people wanted to see, and he trusted her judgement implicitly.

'Are you satisfied, sir?' Henri asked.

He wouldn't be satisfied with anything until Lena was
back in his life, but, until then, this would have to be enough.

'It's time to hit send.'

Henri reached for his laptop. Tapped on the keyboard,
then looked up over the screen. 'It's done. Their Majesties'
private secretary will be—'

'To put it colloquially, *pissed off*, but I don't give a damn.'

If this failed as a broader strategy, he hadn't lost anything.
Lena was still gone. Nothing could hurt him more than he'd
hurt himself on that score, but Gabriel hoped in the process
he might gain her respect. If it succeeded, then he'd freed
himself and his family from a secret that had given power
to a rogue advisor of state, which the man had sought to ex-
ploit through the tabloid media.

With one keystroke of a computer, Gabe had taken the
power back. But that was only the beginning. He had a
plan. One that had taken time and thought. Which would

either be spectacularly successful or leave him shot down in furious flames. He doubted there was a middle ground in this next step, his greatest challenge of all. Making it up to Lena, fighting for her, and bringing her home to his loving embrace.

For ever.

CHAPTER ELEVEN

ISOLOBELLO GLEAMED IN perfection for the royal wedding between Prince Caspar and Princess Priscilla. The capital and every town bedecked with garlands and banners for the event. It was a magnificent morning for a celebration. The sun shone golden in a flawless blue sky. The weather, comfortably warm. Lena stood in the lounge area of her small flat. Television droning in the background to stop her racing thoughts. The churn in her belly as if it were full of snakes. She looked down again at the heavy cream card of an invitation that had come six weeks earlier, delivered to her home by courier.

His Majesty King Constantine
requests the pleasure of the company of
Ms Lena Rosetti
at the marriage of
His Royal Highness Prince Caspar of Isolobello
with
Princess Priscilla of Halrovia

After what had happened between her and Prince Gabriel, she hadn't been sure that her friendship with Cilla would survive. Yet she held the unmistakable evidence that it had in her hands. Whilst photographs she'd seen online from others displaying their invitations in excitement showed their names in calligraphy, hers had been written in the fine, elegant hand she knew to be Cilla's.

It was personal and touching. But still, Lena's heart kicked against her ribs. She took a deep breath trying to settle it. Lena slid the invitation back into her clutch purse with trembling fingers. For a while she hadn't known what to do, but as the RSVP date had approached, she'd found herself accepting the invitation. So here she was, dressed and waiting for her allotted time to leave home for Isolobello's cathedral. The guests' arrival staged to avoid traffic jams in the overflowing city, full of media and visitors wanting to celebrate what had been billed as the wedding of the year.

Yet right in this moment, she wasn't sure she wanted to go. Her teeth worried her lower lip, the fear at seeing Gabriel again almost throttling her. He'd clearly made some changes in his life. For some masochistic reason she hadn't immediately cancelled news alerts for him. The last headline she'd seen, after an important media release...

Heart of a Hero: Prince Gabriel's Dyslexia Revelation Sparks Hope for Others

He'd done it. What she believed was one of the most important things she'd ever suggested to him. It had been at that point she couldn't bear it any more and had shut the alerts down, because he was clearly moving on and so should she.

Lena rubbed at an ache in her chest, refusing to let the burn of tears spill over and ruin her make-up. How could she face him? Sure, he'd sit up front of the cathedral with the other members of royalty, but still… At least she was only invited to the ceremony. The reception was a private family-only affair. All she could do was cross her fingers and hope there was little chance of her catching any more than a glimpse of the man she'd walked away from, breaking her heart in the process.

In the distance the cheers of the crowd rose and fell like the roar of a winter's wind. Ebbing and flowing as some carriage or car paraded down the main street towards the cathedral, which she could see on the television as she'd watched throughout the day. She checked the time. Her car would be here soon enough to take her, once most of the dignitaries had arrived. She still had time to collect her thoughts, rein in her emotions. Get herself in the mood for a day to celebrate love. Something she now understood, deeply and viscerally, that she wanted for herself.

Only the man she wanted it with was unavailable, and not for her.

Lena took a deep breath. It was fine. *She* was fine. What had she expected anyway? A commoner and an illegitimate child, her father unacknowledged. Had she ever really contemplated that one day she might be Queen of Halrovia when things had started with Gabe?

The truth was, for a fleeting moment, she almost had. What she craved was for someone to love *her*, to choose *her*. To see her for who she was and not the family she'd been born into.

When she'd returned home from Halrovia, Lena had sat down to have some hard conversations with her mother. But they were also some of the most real, because of her new understanding of what her mum might have gone through. They'd spoken, and they'd cried. Both of them grieving. She'd admitted what had happened with Gabe, what she'd felt. Lena had expected her mother to berate her choice. Instead, her mother had cupped her cheek and explained to Lena how she'd fallen in love with a man and hadn't thought of the consequences till she'd been in too deep. Too far in love and too lacking in confidence to contemplate life without him. How much she admired Lena for her courage and her self-belief; having the strength to walk away. Then they'd cried some more. So many tears had fallen that day.

But she couldn't stay sad for ever. She had to keep moving. She'd been in a kind of stasis long enough. Whilst her teacher had always said, *'There is a divinity which shapes our ends, rough-hew them how we will'*, Lena realised the flaw in that quote. It removed her agency. She'd spent enough time waiting for the universe to work things out for her. Now she had to drive her own life. Which had led to her seeing a lawyer, as Gabe had suggested, to get her own advice on her father's failure to provide for them. And what she'd learned had changed her and her family's life. That they were entitled to part of the estate. A sizeable part.

So, she'd turned up to her half-brother's office and demanded their share. Not everything they were entitled to, but enough to keep her mother in her home, and her brother in university. As for her, initially she'd balked at taking any money from her father's estate but, as her younger brother had pointed out, neither of them had asked to be born, and some money, whilst not making them rich, gave her choices. She didn't have to work for anyone. She could complete her degree, start her own business. And when the dust settled, that was what she'd do. She'd have what she'd always wanted. An education. Financial security.

And yet it still seemed as if there was something, or someone, missing.

As she stood watching her country's flags fluttering in the breeze out of her window, the clatter of horses' hooves sounded in the distance. That was weird, because the path of the procession to the wedding wasn't close enough to her home to be able to hear the horses. Perhaps they were mounted police patrolling in ceremonial uniform?

'There's something you don't see every day. What are they doing?'

An announcer on the television. She turned and the two people onscreen, a man and a woman, were chuckling.

'Perhaps they've left something behind?' said the man. 'The ring?'

Lena couldn't see what they were laughing at, but surely no one had forgotten the wedding ring. She tried to listen to what the announcers were saying. Something about a carriage turning around. However, the only pictures onscreen were of guests arriving at the cathedral. The announcers said they had a reporter on the ground trying to find out what had gone on, except Lena was distracted by the clatter of hooves becoming louder on the roadway outside her apartment. The rhythm and the sound suggesting horses working in unison, rather than individually.

She went to her window overlooking the cobbled street below as the announcers mentioned something about a residential area and a carriage. In the distance she saw movement, and the reason for the sound became clear. Horses.

Six. Black. Carrying three riders in full livery of red and gold and pulling a gleaming open carriage.

Her heart leapt to her throat, beating a quick and thready rhythm. She stood there gripping the window frame. The wood cool and hard under her fingertips as the carriage came closer and closer. Two men sitting in it. The broad back of one with unruly brown hair and another, whose hair was gold like the sun.

Lena gasped and pulled back. Slamming shut the windows as if trying to lock herself in. She turned to the television as they talked about members of the public calling in saying the landau carriage carrying Aston Lane and Prince Gabriel of Halrovia was travelling through the back streets of the capital to an unknown destination.

It wasn't unknown at all. They were in *her* suburb, on her street.

Lena didn't know what to do, where to go. Her thoughts whirled but none of them made sense. The sound of the hooves echoing off the buildings either side of the narrow street below became louder and louder. Lena wanted to put her fingers in her ears and pretend that this wasn't happening as the hooves clattered, slowed and came to a stop what sounded like right outside her building.

She refused to look out. She stood in the middle of the lounge area of her apartment. Waiting. For what? The building had security. No one could get in. But, she knew, no one would keep out a *prince*. Perspiration beaded on her brow. A trickle ran down the back of her neck as she tried to breathe. The television droning in the background supposing what the Crown Prince of Halrovia was doing. The whole scenario so bizarre and dissonant because she *knew* what he had to be doing.

He was coming to see her.

A knock sounded at the door. She jumped, the sound sharp and urgent. Without her thinking much, her feet took her to the door. Her hands trembling as she undid the chain. Methodically working the locks and opening it.

She gripped the door jamb to keep her upright as the man who had haunted too many of her dreams came into view, in a rush that pushed the breath from her lungs. Her Gabe.

No, *not* hers.

She might have liked to pretend but Prince Gabriel was his country's, and always would be. He'd made it clear that he hadn't considered a future with her. She'd done the right thing and set him free by leaving, as much as he'd freed her in the time they'd been together.

She couldn't look at his face. Not yet. His clothes were easier. He was as perfectly, formally attired as she'd always remembered. More so today in his morning dress. The dark coat, paler grey striped trousers. Cream waistcoat. Soft pink tie…

Oh.

Her lips almost broke into a smile because Pieter would have *hated* it with the power of a thousand suns.

She focussed on the tie of that offending colour for a while, almost afraid to look anywhere else. But she had nothing to fear, not any more. In walking away from him she had shown just how brave she could really be.

'Lena.'

Her name sounded like a benediction. She couldn't help herself. She looked up. To his full lips that had kissed and pleasured her till she'd wept. Heat crept up her throat at the memories. His eyes, the pale blue of melting snow in spring. But even though the colour might have appeared cool, it was only an illusion. Something about them, the look *in* them, blazed like the hottest of summer suns. She didn't know what to say, she could hardly remember how to breathe, so she blurted out the only thing that came to mind.

'Th-they said you might have left something behind—what?'

Gabe's Adam's apple bobbed as his throat convulsed in a swallow.

'You, Lena. Nothing else but you.'

CHAPTER TWELVE

SEEING LENA AGAIN was like a knock to the head. She stood before him, a vision in a silky dress of the softest pink, like the first hint of sunrise. A picture of such perfection that his words had failed. He'd forgotten the effect she had on him. His tongue was tied. She was inside him, had burrowed in deep into his marrow and taken up residence. One look at her in the flesh, rather than the distant and painful memories from the glorious and devastating time together, entrenched Gabe's view. There was no letting her go. He couldn't.

Every official function before Cilla's wedding, he'd known a part of him was missing. Seeing Priscilla, Caspar, Ana and Aston had solidified something he'd resolved weeks before with his press release. Marrying a princess because it was expected of him, *not* marrying for love, was something he could never do. His feelings for Lena would always come first. Even if she refused him today, he'd love her. Which was why he needed to make it up to her with everything he had. Because his life would be meaningless without her.

Lena's eyes widened as she gripped the door jamb till her fingertips paled.

'How did you find me?'

He'd always known where she'd gone. In the time since she'd left Halrovia he'd been driven to ensure she and her family had a home and weren't out on the streets. That there was food on the table, and she wasn't being forced into a situation she didn't want, like marrying. His discreet enquiries had satisfied him that she was okay, giving him time to plan.

'Finding you was the easy part. As for the rest…'

None of that had been easy, but anything was simpler than the days since she'd walked out of Halrovia's palace. Being flayed alive would have been easier than that. Yet for now he had some more pressing matters to deal with. As he stood on her stoop, some doors in the hall of her apartment building had opened. Gabriel accepted that a royal postillion landau carriage parking in the street below would cause a stir, but a few people had begun to peer out at them both. Whilst he could have a conversation with Lena in the hall if that was what she wanted, he preferred a little privacy, where he could try to say the things he needed to get her back in his arms and in his life again.

To let her know how much he loved her.

'May I come inside?' he asked.

'You're on your way to your sister's wedding.'

'And yet here I am, finding I can't go any further.'

'What if you're late?'

'I'll be forgiven.'

By his sisters at least. His parents might never overcome the theatrics, but he didn't care. He'd said enough after his world had imploded the day Lena had left. He liked to believe that his mother and father were taking the time to think about those harsh truths, though he was satisfied to continue communicating with them, private secretary to private secretary, until he had a suitable apology. It was easier, now he'd bought a home away from the palace. The purchase contracts only just settled. Soon he'd be moving.

He hoped to bring Lena home with him.

A few people began pointing phones at Lena's doorway to film what was happening. Whilst he spent his life under constant scrutiny, he wanted to ease Lena into her moment in the spotlight. If he could convince her of the truth of his feelings, today was going to be a big day.

Lena seemed to catch herself, seeing all her neighbours peering at them. The phones pointed their way. She stood back.

'Come inside. Quickly. I don't want to be the story here.'

He stepped over the threshold, and she shut the door gently behind her then turned. In the shock of seeing her again he hadn't noticed how tired she looked. A little like himself. She hid it well under make-up, but it still wasn't enough. And there was something else he noticed about her too. The way she wrung her hands in front of her. Bit into her lip. The look on her face, troubled. He'd done that to her. Failed to realise how tender and soft her heart was. How much his rejection would hurt because of what her father had done to her. In the beginning he'd kidded himself that their secrecy was for her. To protect Lena from the bright lights of media attention when nothing was certain. But that had never been the truth. His deepest confession was that keeping her hidden was entirely selfish.

He'd been trying to come to terms with so many things. Managing the media, sure, but his own feelings. He hadn't understood those at all, when they were now clear and bright like a beacon. He'd been in love with her before he'd even realised, because she saw Gabriel Montroy. A man who wasn't proud or proper or any of those things. He simply *was*.

'Why are you here?' she asked him. 'I don't want to be responsible for holding up your sister's wedding to my future king.'

'As far as I'm concerned, the whole world can wait. Nothing's more important than this, than *you*, Lena.'

A wash of colour flooded her cheeks. 'That's not true.'

'And there lies my greatest mistake.'

Gabe would never stop regretting how uncertain he'd made her. Causing this doubt. Together, he'd not only found someone who saw him, but he'd seen her too. A woman who'd blossomed when given attention. Someone strong. Who could take over the world if she wanted to, because she'd completely taken over his. Every day, every waking thought. All his dreams.

'I have so much to apologise for,' he said. 'Most of all I want to apologise for making you believe that you hadn't become the most important person in my life. That I was in some way embarrassed, and wanted you hidden, when all I should have done was show the world what I saw. How incredible you *are*.'

'But your parents—'

'Need to learn that you were never a whim. I've had strong words with them, my mother in particular, about the things she said. But that's for another day. What I came to tell you was that you're the woman who unlocked my heart. The woman I would give up *everything* for.'

'What do you mean?'

'I have my sister's wedding to attend, but I find I don't want to go.' Lena's eyes widened. Huge pools of blue. A colour he'd missed, craving it over the last few months without her. 'Not without you by my side.'

Lena wished there were something she could hold on to. Anything. She wanted to fall over on the spot. Even though she might have hoped and dreamed, Gabriel stood in a place she'd never believed she'd see him. Her lounge room. On his sister's wedding day. And if she believed her ears, he wanted her to join him as his guest.

Impossible.

'Your parents would never accept me.'

'I don't care about them.'

'You should.'

He frowned, looking confused. But then, he wouldn't understand. He'd been accepted wherever he went.

'They're steeped in tradition, which has locked them in the past. But I've told them that until they've reflected on their behaviour and suitably apologised, there's going to be a distance between us. Though I have little doubt that if they truly came to know you, then they'd love you. As I do.'

'You what?' A sensation burst inside, like a thousand birds taking flight at dawn, singing a joyous song.

He moved forward, towards her. His face beaming like sunshine lighting up the room.

'I love you. I could never marry for duty, because it would eat away at me. I'd come to hate everything and everyone if I was forced to give up on the one person who showed me myself. Who made me better every day. Who brought colour into a world that had been grey. I'd give up everything for you, my place in succession, because you have my heart and no one else will do.'

She froze. Her brain simply couldn't compute what he'd said.

'I—wait. You can't. Give up *being King*?'

'If the only way I can have you is to give up my right to the throne, then that's what I'll do. I'll always choose you.'

'But you'd be an amazing king. What are you talking about? I don't understand.'

The corner of Gabriel's mouth kicked up in a half-smile. It looked entertained, but also sad.

'You would have understood, had I been the man I should have been. Treated you the right way. Fought my parents for you. But I wanted more time to sift through my feelings because they were so unfamiliar. I should have told them that, told you. Stood up for you, for what you meant to me. It's my greatest regret that I didn't. I treated you like your father did, when you're a woman who deserves to shine, not be hidden away. You are not my guilty secret. You're nobody's.'

All her life, she'd been told to stay in the shadows. Not to talk about her father, to say she didn't know, to protect him. To protect her mother. Now Gabe was here. Acknowledging what she'd once craved and dreamed of. Being recognised, being truly seen. Yet in all her dreams, she'd never dreamed of anything like this.

'If I haven't been clear, let me make it plain...' Gabe said, walking towards her. Standing closer. So tall and solid. A man who could take her breath away. Who might even help her shoulder some burdens, as she'd helped him. 'I love you, Lena. There's no one else in the world I want. You already rule my heart. One day, I want you to rule my country by my side. You impressed me *that* much.'

The man she loved, a man who would one day be King,

wanting her to be his queen. Saying he would give it all up for her. *Her*. She'd be thrown into the world's spotlight. There would be no hiding any more.

Lena found she liked that idea, because it gave her Gabe.

'I think I'm tired of hiding. I hid my past from you because I was afraid. I didn't really trust that you wouldn't judge me like others had.'

'I hope you trust me now?'

She nodded. 'I do.'

Gabe took another step forwards, the corners of his lips quirking as if he wanted a smile to break free but wasn't yet sure.

'Then, I'll always work to honour that trust. Come join me at my sister's wedding. Show the world what you mean to me. It seems you're dressed for it.'

Her heart leapt. 'Today?'

'Is there a better time? Cilla did say I could bring a "plus one", as she put it.'

'Where would I even sit at the reception? I have an invitation to the ceremony but you don't just walk into the formal lunch for family.'

'You are invited. You'll be with me. But you're concerned…'

He reached into his coat pocket and slid out a mobile phone. Scrolled. Put the phone to his ear. Lena didn't know who he was calling, but she could hear the murmur of a voice at the other end.

'I know, I'm running a little late. I need you to do something for me. If I bring someone to the reception, make sure there's a place for her?'

Gabe hesitated for a second. More. Lena's heart pounded. What if the answer was no? Then Gabe flinched. Pulled the phone from his ear and held it out. Lena could hear the shrieking, which sounded exuberant rather than angry. After a few moments, Gabe put the phone back to his ear, grinning.

'Yes, it *is* the best thing but don't get too excited. I haven't heard the magic word… But I hope so, too. She just needs to know there'll always be a seat at the table for her… Right. See you soon.'

He slipped the phone back into his pocket. 'It's done, if you want to join me.'

'Who did you speak to?'

'Ana, who passed the news on to Cilla, hence the collective and premature shrieks of joy.'

'Are they premature?'

'You haven't said yes. I understand why you might be reluctant, but I can't be clearer. I love you. I want to spend my life with you. I want to show everyone the woman who found me, who saw me. Who made me a better man. Who'll one day make me a better king.'

Then Gabriel dropped to the floor, down on one knee in front of her. The sight of him so surreal she could hardly believe this wasn't all a dream.

'Would you do me the honour of joining me at my sister's wedding? Of, one day, becoming my wife? Or if you're still not sure, come with me and we can call it a trial period. Test the waters. See if you like it. See if you still like me.'

She looked at him, beaming up at her. His face full of hope. A man who saw her too. The man she loved. The man who said he would give up everything for her, and she believed him.

'Kind of a probation period?'

'Where I get to try and impress you.'

She smiled back at him. 'You don't have to impress me. You already have. And I think we both know there's no point in a probation period when we love each other. We may as well make it official.'

Gabe took her hands in his and smiled right back in a way that pierced her heart with pure joy. 'Then, Lena. Will you marry me, so that we can spend the rest of our lives together, making each other happy? Because I want you, from this day and for ever.'

'Yes. I love you, Gabriel Montroy. The answer is *always* yes.'

Gabe stood and took her into his arms, dropped his lips to her mouth and kissed her, long and deep. As if pouring all of his love into that one moment. Something passionate and endless. The heat of it ignited inside her, the slow burn soon turning into a blazing wildfire as he crushed her to him, and she plunged her hands into his hair. Time lost all meaning now they were together again. After too long and yet not enough they slowly pulled apart, both breathless. Both smiling. Lena drifted her thumb over Gabe's lips, wiping away the lipstick.

'Sealed with a kiss,' she murmured as Gabe cradled her close to his chest.

'And what a kiss it was.'

Lena sighed. It was the kind of kiss stories might be written about. Happily, she now got to write her own.

There was a loud rap at the door.

'Montroy, I don't want to interrupt but we have a wedding to get to and the horses are restless. So are the press who are now surrounding the carriage, asking why we've stopped. What do you want me to tell them?'

'One minute,' Gabe called out, then looked down at her. 'That's Ana's husband. Are you ready to join me?'

'Will Priscilla forgive you for stealing the attention on her wedding day?'

'Always thinking of others. One day I hope to teach you to think of yourself. Do you remember the squeals? As you've heard, she'll be more than happy. She wanted you there. She sent you an invitation. Cilla and Ana will probably try to steal you away from me for all the gossip. Just promise to save me a dance.'

'Every dance is yours.'

'Excellent.' He brushed his lips gently to hers again. 'So, are you ready to…go viral?'

Lena had never been so desperate to take what she wanted. To leap into the limelight, as now. She didn't want to hide any more, she simply wanted to be with the man she loved, and nothing else mattered.

'Can you imagine the headlines?'

'Yes, I can. They'll all say something like… *A Royal Fairy Tale: Prince Finds True Love with His Secret Cinderella.* The moment they see us together they'll be writing how it's the romance of the decade. One that'll enchant and captivate the nation.'

She laughed. 'I love the sound of that.'

'So do I.'

Gabe released her from his arms and took her hand. Threading his fingers through her own. His hold so strong and sure, she knew they'd weather anything so long as they were together. That he'd never let her go.

'Then let's do it,' she said, with her heart full of love. Ready to face the world as they walked hand in hand to the door. Heading into their fairy-tale future together.

EPILOGUE

Two years later

A GENTLE WARM sunshine beamed down as Gabriel and Lena sat in the royal carriage on its procession from Halrovia's cathedral to the palace. Gabe gave a final wave to the jubilant crowd that had lined the streets to celebrate their wedding, before the carriage passed through the palace's iron gates to the mews beyond. It had been two years since Gabe and Lena had returned to Halrovia in the heady days after Cilla and Caspar's wedding reception in Isolobello. On that glorious day they'd laughed and danced and showed everyone how much in love they were. Ever since, no one had doubted he and Lena were destined for one another.

Lena turned to him and smiled. Her diamond tiara, which he'd had specially commissioned for this day, twinkling in the sunlight.

'You look…' Gabe swallowed at the knot that choked his throat. Blinked away the burn in his eyes. His wife was an exquisite woman but today, seeing her walk down the aisle in her wedding dress—a marvel of a white hand-made lace embossed with a pattern of Halrovia's native alpine wildflowers, a cobweb-like veil of tulle trailing behind her—his composure had cracked. She was the only person who could bring him to his knees. Perfect in every way—perfect for him.

She cupped his cheek, her eyes gleaming with tears of her own. 'I've never seen you more handsome. And I've never been happier.'

A flame of warmth kindled deep in his chest. Lena had been accepted by the people of Halrovia with joy and openness. They were simply happy to see their prince happy—nothing else mattered. As he'd promised her, the press had been mostly kind to them and their relationship. It seemed that his earlier disclosure about his dyslexia had worked. His approval had surged. Attempts by the rogue advisor to foment more discord about the royal family had been quickly quelled. He'd lost his power as Gabe had predicted. The final blow had come after a fickle media had turned on him and begun to investigate what appeared to be some questionable financial transactions, leading him to quietly resign from his role with the royal family. All the tabloids were now filled with stories of the public's support and love for the woman who'd stolen Gabe's heart. Only speaking of Lena with praise.

Gabriel took her hand in his, brought it to his mouth. Kissed it. Her engagement and wedding rings glittering in the sunlight. He'd taken time with her to design the perfect ring to honour their love. An oval sapphire the colour of her eyes and the seas around her island home. Flanked by heart-shaped, vibrant yellow diamonds. A representation of the sunshine and light she'd brought to his life. Together, the stones also represented the colours of the Halrovian flag, their life together.

In the beginning, he'd given Lena time. Allowing her to finish her studies. Steadily introducing her to the role she'd one day take up as Queen. She hadn't needed it. Whilst he'd helped her navigate the complexities of royal life, which she'd relished because of her kind and generous soul, it wasn't all one-sided. She'd helped him too, opening him to new possibilities.

'Have you forgiven me yet, for my decision last week?'

Lena pouted, but, from the cheeky twinkle in her eyes, he knew it was all for show. 'I still think you were wrong. The little black schnauzer in the bee suit should have won the pet competition.'

'I still believe the snake was the right choice. The owner had made it a *hat*. I've never seen anything like it. Anyhow, I wanted to prove my personal growth to you by that choice.'

'My darling husband, you still wore a *suit*.' Lena began to laugh. 'But you did work with children and animals and that…was impressive.'

'My darling husband.' How he relished those three words when, for a time after Lena had left him, Gabe had thought he might never be granted the privilege. 'You've always left an impression on me.'

Their carriage pulled to a stop and a member of staff in ceremonial finery opened the door. Gabriel hopped down.

'Are you ready?' he asked.

He and Lena were to be presented on the palace balcony as husband and wife. It was the moment he felt as if he'd been preparing for, for most of his life. Except it took on so much more meaning and import with Lena at his side.

She looked down at him from the carriage and beamed. His love, his princess, his future queen.

'Of course I'm ready. I'm with you.'

He helped her down from the carriage, waiting by her side as her train was adjusted, then offered her his arm as they made their way into the palace. His family and hers had already arrived.

Caspar and Aston had been his best man and groomsman today. Cilla and Ana had been Lena's matron of honour and bridesmaid. It had caused a stir to have a future queen and a princess in those roles, but his sisters were Lena's friends, as their husbands were his, and that made his heart whole.

'Hurry up, you two!' Cilla called out. 'You can't be late for the *world*.'

As far as Gabe was concerned, the world could wait a little longer.

They entered the hall leading to the balcony, where they'd soon formally greet the public as Prince Gabriel and Princess Lena. Husband and wife. As Cilla and Ana went ahead, chatting and catching up now that they lived in different countries, he saw his parents waiting to the side, talking to Lena's mother and brother, both of whom had walked her down the aisle.

It had been a slow repair to his relationship with them. Gabe had been protective of Lena, keeping her away from the King and Queen, even though they'd reached out and asked for another introduction. Small steps had finally led to acceptance; when his parents had realised that only one person would make him happy. As he'd explained, shouldn't that be what any parent wanted for their child? Of course, they'd agreed.

'We're ready when you are,' his private secretary, Henri, said. Since the announcement of his engagement to Lena,

Henri and Pieter hadn't stopped smiling. He'd made many people happy with his choice, and that satisfied him to the depths of his soul.

'I'd like one moment.'

Henri nodded as Gabriel led Lena into a room off the corridor, on the opposite side to the balcony where they'd be presented to Halrovia's people. He shut the door behind them for privacy, but could still hear the rumble of anticipation from the crowd who'd packed the palace forecourt and the main road beyond. All hoping to see their Prince and new Princess, to witness the obligatory kiss.

'Come here.'

Gabe turned and opened his arms. Lena walked straight into them. He relished the feel of her in his embrace. For a few days before their wedding she'd stayed with her mother in one of the royal residences made available for them. He'd missed Lena. Their home felt empty in her absence. It reminded him of how unfulfilled his life had been before she'd burst into it.

'I wanted some time alone with you,' he murmured, 'because today, you're everybody's.'

'No, I'm not,' Lena said. 'I'm yours. Always yours— never forget that.'

'As I'm yours,' he said, smiling, his heart overfull.

'Of course you are. You promised. And I trust you.'

That trust meant *everything* to him. He'd honour it, and never betray it. Lena rested her head on his chest as he held her. She was taller today, wearing heels. He'd caught a glimpse of them in the carriage on the way back to the palace, the sparkle of crystals.

'Tonight…' he said.

'Mmm...?'

'Leave the heels on.'

She gave a low, throaty chuckle and melted further into his body. 'Do you intend to live up to your reputation, Your Royal Hotness?'

'I'll never make you a promise I can't keep.'

She tilted her head up, her pupils wide and dark in the ocean of her eyes. A hint of pink flushed across her cheeks. 'Lucky me...'

'I think I'm the lucky one but let's not argue on our wedding day. Another kiss from my bride?'

Gabe craved this private time before having to share her with the world again. He dropped his mouth to hers, and her lips parted. The kiss tender, languid, full of reverence. Even though they had a whole future ahead of them, they took their time, reconnecting. Learning each other all over again.

Each day was an adventure of discovery with her.

A gentle knock sounded at the door. It was a reminder. For now, they were Halrovia's. At the reception tonight, and afterwards, they could be each other's again. He held out his hand and she took it as they walked back into the hall towards a room with expansive French doors opening onto the balcony, where the rest of the family would shortly gather. As they entered the space, everyone smiled.

'Let's do this,' he said, and Lena squeezed his hand in acknowledgement.

The doors were opened wide allowing the King and Queen through first, followed by the rest of the family as Gabe and Lena held back. The sound of the crowd surged in like an ocean storm, its roar ebbing and flowing.

'Oh. My. Goodness,' she whispered, gripping his hand tighter. 'Listen to everyone.'

Sometimes even he forgot what the crowds could be like from the balcony, but Lena would soon see. Realise how loved she was. It was unavoidable in the face of this.

'It's all for you,' he said as they stepped out into the morning sunshine. A sea of people spread before them, chanting their names.

Lena turned to him and smiled. 'It's for you too, never forget.'

'I know if I do, you'll remind me. Now, shall we give everyone what they've been waiting for?'

Soon, a kiss wouldn't be enough. There was already speculation about a royal pregnancy. He and Lena had spoken privately about giving up contraception for the honeymoon. Perhaps there'd be a royal baby sooner than anyone thought. Whenever it happened, he was ready. In the meantime, he couldn't wait to start trying.

But that was for later, in the quiet of their honeymoon suite.

'I don't believe things could be any better than right now,' Lena said, her voice trembling and thick with emotion.

Gabe understood. He'd never imagined he could have what he'd gained with Lena by his side. His partner. His equal. The woman he loved. 'We've a lifetime yet to come.'

They turned to face each other. Gabe leaned down and kissed her gently on the lips. She placed her hand tenderly on his cheek and kissed back. The cheers of the crowd rushing over them in a tidal wave of joy as they shared the truth of their undying love with the world.

* * * * *